W. Drott
good for adult class
text :
Theo. class
all the class "Dialogue"

Requiem for a Lost Piety

REQUIEM FOR A LOST PIETY

*The Contemporary Search
for the Christian Life*

ethics .

BY EDWARD FARLEY

THE WESTMINSTER PRESS
PHILADELPHIA

LIBRARY OF CONGRESS CATALOG CARD NO. 66–17605

PUBLISHED BY THE WESTMINSTER PRESS ®
PHILADELPHIA, PENNSYLVANIA
PRINTED IN THE UNITED STATES OF AMERICA

to my parents

Raymond Lee Farley
Dora Walker Farley
who
patiently endured and forgave
both the pieties and the impieties
of the author

CONTENTS

PREFACE

Insofar as the following chapters fall together in some sort of unity, the nature of that unity is that of a historical rather than a theological thesis. Perhaps such a distinction is too simple, for this "historical" thesis is not the sort of thesis one usually finds in ordinary history books. If it is history that is being undertaken here, surely it is a very peculiar kind of history. One reason for the peculiarity is that the historical object itself is peculiar: the history under investigation here is a certain moment in the history of the church. "Church" does not mean simply the obvious empirical and institutional entity that is the object of sociological and historical inquiries. The "church" of the present inquiry is the more theologically determined entity, a people whose existence and unity is provided by God himself. Already we are operating with a faith category; hence, the peculiarity of the history informed by that category.

Furthermore, the way we approach this peculiar historical object, the church, is also not history in the usual sense, for that approach is determined from the very first by "faith categories." We are, in this study, observing that something is happening to the "piety" of a particular (Protestant) church. The thesis therefore assumes certain *theological* distinctions between faith and piety, genuine and pseudo piety, Christian piety and relative historical forms of piety. Thus, while this thesis is primarily about a certain historical and cultural state of affairs, the lens through which we are looking is a theological one. If it is history that is being done here, it is theological history: historical description that at the same time is theological criticism.

And now two disclaimers. Some readers may find material here that seems to be new. Some may be surprised and even shocked at the criticisms and treatment of the traditional Protestant version of the Christian life. Yet I would not want to give the impression that this is a new or original work. Almost all the theological and cultural observations made in these chapters can be found in the literature of theology and Christian ethics of the past theological generation. My own work therefore has been more that of a collector than a creator. If there is any originality at all, it would reside in bringing these criticisms of Protestant piety together into one picture, and then drawing a certain conclusion about our present situation. But for the most part, I am simply drawing on the writings of such men as Reinhold Niebuhr, H. Richard Niebuhr, and Dietrich Bonhoeffer.

The second disclaimer is that the present study does not pretend to be a technical, scholarly, or scientific work in the field of theological ethics or theological history. To the extent that this is the case, professional historians will see immediately how general is the thesis and how sparse the evidence. The specialist in theological ethics will recognize how incompletely and imprecisely faith and piety are described. At this point, I can only acknowledge that such is the case. Yet I must at the same time say that this is meant to be a serious work. As a piece of writing, it is addressed not to the professional scholar but to human beings who might find themselves in the transitional moment and in the vacuum of piety that this book attempts to portray. Hence, while the work may lack an extensive apparatus of historical documentation and theological demonstration, I hope that the sketch is

drawn clearly enough so that most people who examine it will
recognize in it something of their own experience. Hence,
direct description functions to replace more formal kinds of
evidence.

What is the purpose of this work about the displacement of
traditional Protestant piety with some strange-looking substitutes? The undertaking is not meant to be simply a smash-
ing of idols. I am quite serious about the aspect of faith that
gets expressed in concrete and unified patterns. In other
words, I am quite serious about the sort of thing we find in a
Francis of Assisi, John Wesley, or Reinhold Niebuhr—i.e.,
certain "styles" or concretizations of the Christian life. There
was a time in Protestantism when Protestant faith itself put
forth not only a doctrine but also a fairly clear and specific
pattern of the Christian life. This is what I am calling in
these chapters "Protestant piety." Although Protestantism as
a historical community still exists, this pattern of the Christian life does not. Yet many Protestants are able to act out a
kind of make-believe, pretending in their verbal and emotional lives that the traditional pattern still exists. The concrete styles and modes of life that now make up Protestant
churchly and religious life are still an odd assortment of all
sorts of strange and in some cases idolatrous things. Furthermore, the make-believe that nothing has happened prevents
the question of the Christian life from being raised in an
effective way. Like the Emperor in Andersen's fairy tale, many
Protestants are pretending that they are decked out in a
splendid array of Christian virtues and acts, when they are
actually naked, or are wearing the tattered clothing of a
tramp. This book has no great new piety to offer. (The author
is not in the clothing business.) But it does try to air a problem—the decline and fall of Protestant piety in its Victorian
forms.

I would like to say at this point that most of these chapters
were originally worked out for the "Focus" section of *Cross-*

roads, published by the Board of Christian Education of The United Presbyterian Church U.S.A. Therefore I would express my gratitude to Dennis Shoemaker of *Crossroads* (and to others in the Board of Christian Education), with whom the project was originally conceived and whose editorial hand is apparent in the present work.

Introduction

THE SERIOUS BUSINESS
OF CHRISTIAN PIETY

It is becoming clearer every day that the most urgent problem besetting our Church is this: How can we live the Christian life in the modern world?

—*Dietrich Bonhoeffer*[1]

This book is about something called piety. This, in itself, is sufficient reason for the reader to throw the work down and look for something useful, pleasant, or meaningful to do. The very word "piety" gives us (including the author) the creeps. Why, then, in the name of all that is sensible, write a whole book about it? Well, we need some word to describe what the book is about, and the other words available ring just as dead as "piety." We could, of course, invent a word, such as *urgluid* or *pifflism*, but that would only be more confusing. Besides, our very reactions to the word "piety" (feelings of nausea, shoulder shrugs, sneers, and yawns) are symptoms of what has now happened. And that is what this book is about: what has happened in contemporary Protestantism to the Christian life, and to its . . . piety!

The Concreteness of Faith

When we use such expressions as "the Christian religion," "the Christian faith," and "Christianity," what sort of things are we talking about? Do they stand for scientific theories or discoveries such as the theory of relativity or the expanding universe? Apparently not. While "the Christian faith" may have its theoretical or belief aspect, theory or belief is not the whole story. "The Christian faith" stands for a power effective in human lives. Wherever this faith is present, it operates not merely in minds but in the stuff of which our lives are made: feelings, decisions, responses, actions, enterprises, purposings, and the like. The Christian faith is not merely the belief that God is a worshipful being; it is also the worship of that being. The Christian faith is addressed not only to the question, What must I believe? but also, What must I be and do?

This means that we have not finished interpreting the Christian faith or the gospel when we have set forth various doctrines. Interpreting the gospel also means interpreting its demand for obedience, its pressure on us to be this and not that, to do this and not that. Having admitted this, we must face the fact that interpreting the gospel as a pressure on us in the specific situations of our lives has not received the same attention as the interpretation of doctrines. The question of what I am to be and do is usually not asked as consciously and explicitly as the question, What am I to believe? In spite of this, Christians in every age have always attempted to place their lives (their decisions, values, etc.) under the power of the gospel. Interpreting the gospel, they fought with kings, marched on crusades, meditated in lonely caves, lived in monasteries, prayed at mealtimes, and joined in racial demonstrations. Being and acting out of the gospel has always taken place at the most concrete, specific levels of human life, giving rise to total patterns of life. Attempting to be and act out of the gospel has produced the Franciscan monk, the

medieval mystic, the American Puritan, and the enthusiast
for Christian Endeavor.

While life itself is what most specifically expresses this
being-and-acting interpretation of the gospel, such patterns
and types of living also have their verbal expressions. Mysticism had its writings, and so did Puritanism. "Christian
ethics" is usually the name given to the attempt to inquire
into or express the interpretation of the gospel at the level of
actual human life.

The Christian faith is itself a "life" phenomenon. Something about the Christian faith makes it impossible for it to
be excluded from the concrete levels of human decision and
attitude. Or, to put it another way, faith cannot help expressing itself, set itself forth in the actual activities and attitudes
of the faithful person. Thus it would be accurate to say that
to the degree to which a person's concrete life is ordered,
effected, oriented by the faith, to that degree he is called
religious, devout, spiritual, pious, "Christian." Faith is expressed in voting, relaxing, being married, eating and drinking, attending or not attending committee meetings. Faith
tends to put forth patterns of action that affect all levels of
the human being: innermost attitudes; external actions, including both creative and novel actions as well as regular
habitual actions; responses to things, including critical responses, joyous responses, and angry responses.

Our first reaction to this might be to remember that faith
is merely an invisible and inward sort of reality, since it is a
gift of God, a response to God, and also a relation to God.
We cannot help also remembering that we are told that our
"light" should shine before men, that those in the Kingdom
are known by their fruits, and that those who claim to love
God but who hate their brothers are simply liars. Faith apparently has also an outward and visible aspect. But why?

Why is the Christian faith like this? What is there about
the Christian faith that makes it so all-pervasive, so concrete?
The answer lies in the nature of faith itself. If faith is a situa-

tion of being laid hold of by the good news of Jesus Christ, if faith is the situation of being forgiven by God, we are freed to live before God, not merely in guilt or cynicism, but as his sons. Forgiveness, then, sets us free, but this freedom is freedom not *from* God's Word, but for obedience *to* God's Word. In the questions about what to do and be, faith cannot ignore God's Word.

What, Me Pious?

Faith not only is something that presses into the realm of concrete acts and attitudes. Such acts and attitudes tend to fall into a pattern. In other words, not only the beliefs and doctrines of the Christian faith tend to have a unity, but the interpretation of the gospel as a clue to our being and doing also tends to have a unity. Everyone sees some things as more important than other things in the gospel. Furthermore, we tend to take one thing and make that the basic clue to what it means to live the Christian life. For some, the habits and acts of the Christian life are unified and ordered under prayer; for others, the imitation of Christ and Charles Sheldon's question, "What would Jesus do?" are decisive. For still others, the Christian life means essentially tough-minded, fist-clinched battling in the social and cultural crises of the time.

Such a pattern or unity of our acts and attitudes arises for several reasons. Because the foundation of it all is an interpretation of the gospel, that interpretation itself tends toward a pattern. If, on the one hand, we interpret the gospel as essentially a power or presence that produces certain religious feelings inside us, then our concrete living of the gospel will be a search for whatever produces those feelings. If, on the other hand, we see the gospel as a power working to transform human society, working for justice and human welfare, our concrete acts will reflect a pattern unified by that theme.

Another feature of the Christian life tends to produce a unity or pattern. "Being and doing" imply a goal, even as does "interpreting the gospel." The picture here is that of a march, a moving forward. Quite properly, we can ask of our acts and attitudes arising out of the gospel, "What is the point?" *For what* a life of prayer, *for what* work in a political party, *for what* honesty and selflessness? The Christian life itself, life free for the Word of God, implies some goal, however we spell it out. What do the attitudes and acts of the Christian life gain for us? Heaven? Salvation? Peace with God? A Christian and godly character? Happiness and well-being? Naturally, they will also secure things that are ends in themselves, such as social justice. Yet, insofar as the gospel is behind our doing of such things, a motive, a goal is implied that is more than just the specific end attained.

Perhaps we are ready now to look again at this word "piety." I am using it to denote *that which unifies the specific acts and attitudes of the Christian life. A person's piety is a pattern of being and doing that arises out of a specific interpretation of the gospel.* Insofar as several such patterns might conceivably be present in a person's actions, we could speak of several pieties. If a person sees all the attitudes and acts of the Christian as being unified by worship and prayer, his piety would be a *prayer* piety. If the goal is attained by self-denial, discipline, even self-punishment, then it is an *ascetic* piety. Sometimes a whole period of the church has its own "piety," as in the Middle Ages or in Colonial America. Therefore, we speak of an ascetic piety or piety of self-discipline in monastic orders, where life was organized around a personal discipline designed to bring the "flesh" and the passions under control and to order the mind toward God. Closely related would be a *mystical* piety, where life's acts and attitudes are ordered as a means to the vision of God and the contemplation of his presence. Insofar as Roman Catholicism and Protestantism have overall ways of looking at the Christian life that form patterns and unities, we can speak of Roman Catholic piety or Protestant piety. Roman Catholic piety is a sacramental piety where the sacraments, especially

the Blessed Sacrament or Eucharist, are channels of grace
and power to renew and purify the Christian man constantly.

It should be clear by now that piety in this sense is inevitable to faith. Insofar as faith always exists in the concrete
details and acts of human life, and insofar as such are informed at all by the ground of faith, the gospel, there will be
some patterns or unities in these acts, and accordingly, pieties.

Where We Are Not for Sale

We are now in a position to elaborate our definition of
piety. We have already described piety as a "pattern of being
and doing that arises out of a specific interpretation of the
gospel." Insofar as such a pattern is rooted in the gospel, a
piety functions also as a norm or ideal pattern. We could,
therefore, say that a piety is *that which gives a whole set of
actions its foundation, its justification.* A piety, therefore, is
a *pattern* of our actions and thoughts insofar as we look at it
from the outside as something merely to describe. It is also an
ideal or normative pattern that justifies such acts and
thoughts, insofar as we look at it from the inside, as something grounding *our* expressions of faith. When the monk
attempts to justify why he joined a monastery, why he ad-
heres to its discipline, why he follows a regular round of
prayers, that which brings all this together and shows what it
is for and why it is important is his *piety.* In this case it is
the monastic way of describing the goal of the Christian life
and the means to that goal.

And now, some clarifications.

1. Because a person's piety is that to which he appeals to
justify what he does or is or ought to be, we might describe
it as something the person takes most seriously—the point at
which, when he is scratched deeply enough, he yells in protest
or the point at which he is not for sale. Up to that point, the
person can nod in polite social agreement, shrug his shoul-

ders, or tolerantly explore. But when his piety is touched, that which really makes him tick, which gives meaning and justification to his most serious acts and thoughts, then he reacts differently. Here we have the hard core that cannot be molded or prodded into something else. Here we have that which he will not sell, that which, when attacked, provokes defense.

2. Piety, in this sense, need not be anything particularly religious. Secular or nonreligious pieties abound everywhere, and the actual stuff of which our lives are made includes a complex tangle of both secular and religious pieties. An example of a "secular" piety might be a scholar's attitude toward his own work and its foundations. He may be the most open and tolerant person on every subject in the world until it is suggested that knowledge itself is not worthwhile. Then he screams.

Other nonreligious pieties might be democracy, togetherness, or being educated. A secular piety would simply be a foundation of a set of acts or attitudes that has no peculiarly religious reference. Secular piety, in this sense, is not necessarily bad or evil, for surely there are many legitimate activities that need no "religious" foundation or justification. Furthermore, it is crucial that we get this notion of a secular piety into the picture here at the beginning, for part of the total thesis is that traditional religious pieties have now been replaced by secular pieties. Many traditional religious words and phrases now stand for what are in content, secular pieties. This means that the Christian faith either has a problem on its hands or else it is superfluous.

3. Even as a piety might be secular or religious, so it might also be good or bad. Piety is an inevitable thing and, in an ideal sense, a good thing. However, because it does rise out of an *interpretation* of the Christian faith, it is not inevitably a good thing. The faith can be interpreted erroneously, irresponsibly—even demonically. We have, then, the possibility

of "pieties," that is, foundations of certain patterns and unities in our acts which pretend to express faith, but which con-
tradict faith and the gospel that is its ground.[2] Here, then, it
becomes clear that this use of the word "piety" as a "neutral"
pattern, something that can be good or bad, is a departure
from the traditional meaning of the word. When our forefathers described a person as "a pious man," they meant,
roughly, what we would mean by calling someone "religious."
They were trying to say that this person's concrete life exem-
plified the goals and values of religion. He attended church,
tithed, observed the Sabbath, etc. Piety, in this sense, was
inevitably something good. But as the word is being used in
these chapters, piety is only, in the ideal sense, something
good. As the ideal pattern unifying our being and doing, it
is something good. As the *actual* pattern that we come to
have, it only approximately reflects that ideal, hence may be
erroneous, superstitious, or disobedient. The same division
holds also for the secular pieties in that both the tyrant and
the devoted statesman may have their pieties, their justifications. Traditionally, the only alternatives were piety and impiety. Piety, therefore, was a word like "justice," meaning
something good and to be desired. In these chapters it is a
more neutral word, such as "act," and can be either good or
bad. Yet how can this be? If piety is, by definition, a pattern
unifying the expressions of *faith,* how can it be bad? Perhaps
our either-or language is misleading at this point. The expressions of faith are always filtered through our humanity,
which means our imperfect knowledge, our corrupted wills,
our inability to do and be the absolutely perfect. An expression of faith is, therefore, never an absolutely pure response,
a mere reproduction of God's own being or doing, nor need
it be mere disobedience. Rather than being simply good or
bad, such expressions (and the patterns or pieties that unify
them) are more or less adequate, more or less obedient.

4. If "piety" is to be used in this way, it should also be
clear that any one person will have many pieties, and these

will not necessarily be consistent with one another. Mixed up in our consciousness and subconscious are all sorts of justifications, some secular, some religious, some good, some superstitious, some perverse. At least, if we were doing psychological analysis, this, it seems, is what we would find. However, insofar as a person's actual decisions and acts are expressions of faith, some sort of unity will be present. And it is that unity, piety in that sense, that is the subject of this inquiry.

5. If a piety is a foundation, a ground of a defense or justification, a unifying basis of our acts, then it is not so specific as an act or thought or attitude or even habit, such as church-going, or praying; nor is it so broad as the gospel or the Word of God. But the situation is never one of appealing directly to God or to the gospel to justify an act. Instead, we appeal to Scripture, or we claim that it is "the Christian thing to do," or we cite some principle, such as selflessness, or being a stumbling block to our brother. Therefore, in between God and our concrete acts stands what I am calling a piety, which, when taken seriously, gives rise to certain specific acts, directions, or negotiations. Examples of such in-between pieties are:

Selfless motivation is the only Christian motivation.
Following in the footsteps of Jesus gives us the clue to the Christian life.
Worldly and bodily pleasures comprise the chief temptations and obstacles to the Christian life.
The Bible provides us with a clear set of rules for Christian living.

The thesis of the following chapters is simply this: *Most of the pieties that made up traditional Protestant piety are now meaningless to the contemporary Protestant Christian.* The language and the vocabulary of such piety have become empty and hollow. Terms such as "godliness," "sobriety," "a holy life," "Christian character," "Christian principles," "family

altar," "following Jesus," "spiritual," "witnessing for Christ,"
"taking up the cross," "setting an example," "developing
Christian virtues"—all these words and phrases are now, for
the most part, empty clichés. But according to one of the
parables of Jesus (Luke 11:24-26), the Christian can never be
merely an empty house. New occupants, even if they are
demons, move in. Traditional Protestant piety being now
gone with the wind, new pieties are moving in. Faith must
express itself in some concrete way, and many are they who
have ready answers for that impulse. The result is that faith
leaps after concrete expressions that are strange to it and con-
tradictory to it. The contemporary Christian, therefore, seems
ready to listen to and obey almost any voice if only the voice
tells him what to do. And the voices are legion: fanatical
patriotism, fake psychological gimmicks to get mental peace,
dozens of church-renewal schemes, "prophetic" cynicism and
criticism of everything in the church (implying this is the
concrete way to be and do and feel as a contemporary Christian), complicated suburban church programs with endless
meetings and activities, all justified because this is what
Christians do. Therefore, in future chapters, I should like
to explore the main features of Protestant piety, some reasons
why it has collapsed, and some of its contemporary substitutes. Then I should like to look at the problem of the contemporary Protestant Christian in the light of all this.

The reader may follow the argument of the following chapters if we pursue at this time a few basic distinctions, and, in
the light of such, restate the thesis of the chapters in summary
form. I tried to say previously that a piety was simply a *pattern* that united and justified various acts, thoughts, and attitudes in which faith is expressed. At this point a distinction
may be helpful. Wherever piety is genuine, such a pattern
will be comprised of both *relative* and *nonrelative* aspects. A
piety will be *relative* (varying, changing) in the sense that the
way faith expresses itself in different times and situations

changes constantly. It is natural and legitimate that Christians in the early church, in the Middle Ages, and in the twentieth century act and think and respond to their situations in different ways. Responses to the crises of the thirteenth century cannot be the same as the responses appropriate to the twentieth century. We might call this relative or historical aspect of piety *historical piety*. The particular piety under examination in these chapters is one historical piety, namely, Protestant piety.

Yet insofar as piety (the pattern of the expression of faith) is *Christian* piety, something rooted in the gospel of Jesus Christ, there will also be a *nonrelative* aspect in every piety. I mean by this simply that there are certain marks of the Christian life that are always present wherever faith exists, which marks are expressed in being and doing. For instance, love (agape) will always mark the life and expressions of faith. The specific historical form such love will take will vary (what it means to *love* human beings in the inner city, in a Puritan village, and in a monastery). Insofar as there is a part of theology called Christian ethics, and insofar as it has a stable object of inquiry, that object would be this nonrelative aspect of piety. The material of the very last chapter is a study of piety in this sense, this universal, unchanging structure of the Christian life.

This distinction should help clarify the thesis of these chapters. The thesis is that one *historical* piety (Protestant piety) is passing off the scene. The thesis is not that Christian faith, Christianity, or Christian piety are passing away. There are those in our time who rather confidently proclaim that Christian faith itself has gone, that we live now in a "post-Christian era." I would not want to go that far. As I look at the evidence, it seems to say that a certain historical form of Christian piety (Victorian Protestant piety) is going. Faith itself remains, searches for, and in part finds new forms—some idolatrous, some innocuous, and some seemingly genuine.

But at the level of one overall historical piety unifying Protestantism, there seems now to be merely a vacuum. Whether this is a good thing or a bad thing remains yet to be considered.

In the year 1830 there appeared the third edition of a book with a title that would make many twentieth-century church people smile in amused perplexity: *Advice to a Young Christian on the Importance of Aiming at an Elevated Standard of Piety*. This book was written by a Village Pastor, with an Introductory Essay, by the Rev. Dr. Alexander, of Princeton, New Jersey.

The work is only a typical example of many such writings by Protestants. The subtitle of Richard Baxter's monumental *A Christian Directory: or, a Sum of Practical Theology, and Cases of Conscience* (1673) is: "Directing Christians, How to Use Their Knowledge and Faith; How to Improve All Helps and Means, and to Perform All Duties; How to Overcome Temptations, and to Escape or Mortify Every Sin." In other words, Protestantism, like Catholicism, has its own "piety," its own version of the concreteness of faith. A special vocabulary expresses this Protestant piety in such words as "devout," "godliness," "holy living," "sobriety," and "Christian character."[3]

But can we speak of one Protestant piety? Must we not, rather, talk about many Protestant pieties? We can list the pieties that express major periods of Protestant history, such as Puritan piety, Victorian piety, or social gospel piety; or the pieties that are related to denominational traditions, such as Lutheran piety, Methodist piety, and sect-type or Pentecostal piety. Such variations must undoubtedly be acknowledged. However, a general pattern persists through all these "Protestant pieties." We find in this pattern several fundamental motifs or themes common to Methodists and Presbyterians, and common to the various periods of Protestant faith. Therefore, Protestant piety, as I am using the term, is not limited to the piety of the classical or formative periods of Protestantism, such as early Calvinism or even seventeenth-century Puritanism. Protestant piety means a way of interpreting the Christian life that had its beginning in the Reformation, but that picked up various emphases and themes in the post-Reformation centuries. Protestant piety, therefore, is a conglomeration of themes about the Christian life. Some come from ancient Catholic Christianity, some from Luther and Calvin, some from the "Pietism" of Philipp Jacob Spener and John Wesley, some from frontier revivalism.[4] All these together produced a "Protestant piety," an expression of faith in concrete attitudes and acts, duties and disciplines.

PART I

*The Marks of
Protestant Piety*

Chapter One

THE PIETY OF THE SACRED PAGE

Don't blame him. Blame our dead goodness. Holy books, holy pictures, a subscription to the Altar Society. Do you think if she had come into a house where there was love, she wouldn't have hesitated, thought twice.

—*Graham Greene*[5]

For Protestant piety the Christian life is life according to the Sacred Page, the Holy Bible. To Thomas' question, "Lord, we do not know where you are going; how can we know the way?" Protestant piety points to the Book. Thus every Presbyterian minister affirms at his ordination that the Bible is "the only infallible rule of faith and practice." This seems to suggest that the Bible, as a *rule* of *practice,* contains prescriptions that tell us (infallibly) what we are to be and do. Presumably a person can go to the Book (much the same way a realtor consults the city's housing code) to find out whether or not he is allowed to work on Sunday, get a divorce, wear a hat in church, or sue a fellow Christian. If this is the case, living under the rule of God *means* living under the rule of the Book. What God says and what the Book says are synonymous. The words of the Book are simply the words of God.

Given such an identification, we are not surprised to find Protestant piety claiming that the Book is "divine." "Holy

Bible, book divine, Precious treasure, thou art mine." As
divine, the Book itself becomes, like the sacred relics of
Catholicism, the object of veneration or devotion. Hymns are
sung not only to God but to the Book.

> Book of books, our people's strength,
>   Statesman's, teacher's, hero's treasure,
> Bringing freedom, spreading truth,
>   Shedding light that none can measure;
> Wisdom comes to those who know thee,
>   *All the best we have we owe Thee.*[6]

Since the Bible is something "divine," something we can
"hymn," we can quite properly speak about it in the same
way we speak about God, as a fountain and source of
strength; for instance, from *Advice to a Young Christian:*
"To this fountain of light and life, let us then daily resort.
Here is the healing influence. Here is the pool of Bethesda.
Here abounds consolation for the afflicted. Here hope dwells
to cheer and to guide."[7] When we sing to and talk about the
Bible the same way we sing to and talk about God, we have
done with the Bible the same thing we accuse Catholics of
doing with saints and relics. We venerate as divine something
other than God himself.

Some people may object that Luther and Calvin would
never have ascribed "divinity" to the Bible, endowing it with
an attribute of God himself. In general such a disclaimer is
correct. It simply helps us to point out the crucial distinction
between Protestant *theology* and Protestant *piety.* As in
Catholic piety, many beliefs, mind-sets, attitudes, etc., which
occur in the Protestant cultus and culture have no "official"
or confessional standing. Therefore, it is important to remember that what we are studying in these chapters is not the
formal and intellectual world of Protestant theology, but
the more informal and concrete world of Protestant life.
Needless to say, traditional Protestant theology is partly re-

sponsible for Protestantism's viewing of the Bible as a divine object. Its claim that the Bible was errorless in every respect, the very words of God, and its consequent procedure of "proving" statements simply by appealing to the infallible Book, served as crucial foundations of the piety of the Book.

Some Negative Thinking About Book Piety

This piety of the sacred page which views the book as a source of prescriptions clearly telling us what to do and be and which venerates the book as a cultic object of devotion is, theologically speaking, no longer possible. The reason it is no longer possible is not that skepticism has destroyed the authority of the Scriptures; rather, such piety is a mixture of ignorance, superstition, and idolatry. It reflects ignorance because an actual understanding of what the Bible itself *is* renders impossible the "law code" use of the Bible. It takes only a brief and superficial examination of the Bible to see that in its totality it is not a law code. At best it contains a few law codes, the majority of which are ignored by Protestant piety! Therefore, it cannot be used or cited as a law code. This means that its authority is not distributed in every verse the way authority is distributed throughout a legal code. Its authority is located in that which makes Scripture Scripture, namely, the "story" that centers and climaxes in Jesus Christ. Scripture in its totality is the "story" in which are found basic pictures or images (such as man as sinner, the hope of resurrection) and historical events (such as the exodus or the crucifixion) through which the "story" is made clear.

If this is what Scripture *is*, then to justify an action by citing Scripture is simply a superstition and a magical (and therefore pagan) use of Scripture. For example, one hears that we should be embalmed because Jesus was embalmed, that we should not work on Sunday because ancient Jews did not work on Saturday, and that in every situation of conflict we should "turn the other cheek." When we think about it, we realize that no one ever consistently uses Scripture in these ways. Our appeals are always highly selective. We cite the Commandment (Eighth) about stealing, but ignore the Commandment about resting on the Sabbath. We cite the Commandment about the Sabbath, but not the rest of the law code of which the Ten Commandments are a summary. We adhere to the way Jesus was buried, but forget about dozens of other ancient Jewish customs. We legalize one part of the Sermon on the Mount, but conveniently ignore other parts.

The more serious problem with the piety of the Book is its idolatry. We sometimes hear a plaintive and fearful little wail that declares, "If a single mistake is found anywhere in the Bible, I shall lose my faith." Such a remark makes it unmistakably clear what the object of that faith is, namely, the Book, or some human theory about the Book and its inspiration. When God himself and only God himself is the object and the ground of faith, what could remove him? If an error in the Bible could cause a person to lose his faith in God, surely that makes God and the Bible the same thing. Logically, then, if what the Bible says and what God says are identical, the last time God spoke was when the Bible was written. God apparently wrote the Bible and died, or went to sleep! Such a "Book-God" resembles the Canaanite deities whom Elijah ridiculed as perhaps having gone on holiday or having fallen asleep. (I Kings 18:27.)

Some Second Thoughts

Actually, such theological criticism of the piety of the Book is rather superfluous. Criticism or no criticism, such an attitude toward the Book is, for the most part, gone. Pictures of the father reading the Bible daily with the family, Bible-reading and study as a regular exercise of the Christian life, "learning the Bible at Mother's knee"—all sound quaint to the modern ear, memories of a bygone era. What do we have instead? Occasionally, the superstitious and idolatrous literalism is transferred to another document, such as the American Constitution. This then is read literalistically, is applied without interpretation, and, above all (like the words of God), must never be changed. But the more general transition in the churches is the transformation of the piety of the Book into Bible *study* in the church. We study in groups the history of Hebrew religion, the missionary journeys of Paul, and Johannine theology. This means that our basic relation to the Bible is an intellectual one. We gather information from it about the Hebrews, Jesus, and Paul.

But we must ask again, Is this what the Bible *is?* Is there some sense in which it is the Word of God? Is there any sense in which we can legitimately bring to the Scriptures our questions about what we should be and do? Did not Protestant piety express a genuine insight into the Christian life in its stress on the Bible as a "fountain of life and light"? And if, as Luther says, the Bible is the cradle in which Christ lies, dare we approach it merely as an object of study?

Chapter Two

JESUS WITHOUT HIS TITLE

A little talk with Jesus puts it right, all right.

—*Quoted in R. A. Knox,* Enthusiasm[8]

We move now onto very dangerous ground. Another way to designate the standard of obedience that prescribes what we shall do and be is to point to Jesus. The Christian life is not merely life under the rule of the Bible. It is "living for Jesus," who "leadeth me: O blessed thought," "since Jesus is my Friend." When such a motif dominates the way we see the Christian life, Christianity becomes a Jesus cult. When this is the case, the word "God" and the word "Jesus" stand for the same thing. Therefore, obeying God *means* obeying Jesus. Turning to God as our fortress and our strength *means* turning to Jesus. Worshiping and praying to God *means* worshiping and praying to Jesus. There seem to be two major ways the Jesus cult expresses itself and thereby describes the Christian life. The one regards Jesus as a new law. Instead of the law of Moses, Christians follow the law (teachings) of Jesus or the law which is Jesus. The other focuses on a personal relation to Jesus as comprising the Christian's relation to God.

"What Would Jesus Do?"

The above phrase calls to mind one of the more sentimental expressions of the Jesus cult, Charles Sheldon's *In His Steps*. A less sentimental expression of the same thing is the classic of medieval Christendom, *The Imitation of Christ,* by Thomas à Kempis. The picture of the Christian life suggested by these phrases is the picture of Jesus going ahead and the Christian following behind, doing what he did, thinking what he thought, obeying each of his teachings as if it were a legal code. "Where He leads me I will follow," as the hymn goes.

All this rings (or reeks) with piety. At the same time it also reeks with deception. What is it about Jesus that we are going to regard as our standard, our law, our rule? Is the *course of his life* our standard? Obviously not. Jesus had his own Messianic mission, but that mission is not ours. We are not called to be itinerant preachers, with disciples, dying a criminal's death at the end. We are called to live in our own world, according to our gifts, skills, and opportunities as politicians and housewives and plumbers. Are Jesus' *decisions* to be our rule? Again, obviously not. His decisions make sense only in relation to his mission and to specific incidents. We could never exactly duplicate any situation in which Jesus stood (as when the children approached him, or when the woman was accused of adultery). Therefore, we could never be sure that the decision he made in his situation should be duplicated for our own.

Perhaps Jesus' *teachings* are to be our standard and rule. If we follow this line, we should be aware that his teachings, the majority of insights in his parables and discourses, are almost never repeated in the rest of the New Testament. When apostles such as Paul talked about the gospel, when they summarized what the Christian faith was all about, they did not repeat Jesus' teachings. More serious is the fact that the nature of Jesus' teachings prevents them from being clear or applicable standards. Some are so specific that they pertain only to a very ancient or very rare situation, such as Jesus' words about fasting, or not refusing those who want to borrow from us (Matt. 5:42). The problem is further complicated when we realize that the majority of Jesus' teachings are found also in rabbinic Judaism and various Jewish sects of the time; that contemporary New Testament scholars have tremendous difficulty separating Jesus' teachings from the editing and confessing of the primitive church; that only a very arbitrary and subjective act can isolate Jesus' teaching as *the* rule from the rest of the New Testament. Most seriously of all, we must ask whether or not Jesus *is* our new law or standard. Is not Jesus rather *the Christ*? Does not the coming of the Christ signify something more than just a new Sinai? In restricting Jesus to a standard or rule, are we not closing our eyes to his real mission and meaning, the good news, the revealing of God, the declaration of forgiveness, the cross and resurrection?

Idolatry of the Second Person

Secondly, the Jesus cult conceives of the Christian life as a personal and intimate (almost cuddly) relation to Jesus. Now, we could rightly reply that Christians regard Jesus as divine and therefore such a relation is quite justified. But such would not accurately express the piety of the Jesus cult. In Jesus piety, Jesus is not only divine; "God" means Jesus. H. Richard Niebuhr thus accuses the Jesus cult of turning Christian faith into a "Christian religion for which Jesus Christ in isolation is the one object of devotion and in which his own testimony, his very character, his Sonship, his relation to the One with whom he is united, are denied."[9] The Jesus of the Jesus cult is not, let us be clear, Jesus Christ. He is an ancient Jew who did and said certain things, a sort of bearded movie star to whom it is quite appropriate to sing,

"Then, while leaning on Thy breast, May I hear Thee say to me, 'Fear not, I will pilot thee.' " Or, "In His arms He'll take and shield thee, Thou wilt find a solace there."

When the Christian life becomes an admiring or worshipful relation to the man Jesus, it deserves the description that is sometimes made—the idolatry of the Second Person—for the Jesus cult tends to eliminate God for the sake of Jesus. It exchanges the relation to God for the relation to Jesus and the worship of God for the worship of Jesus. Therefore, God is not worshiped as *God:* as Father, Son, and Spirit. Hence God is rejected. Furthermore, Jesus is rejected, since he is not approached as Jesus the Christ, the one *sent* by God, in whom God was in some way present, and by whom God is made known.

But we must say again that such theological criticism of this aspect of Protestant piety is also superfluous. The sect groups may still reflect something of the Jesus cult; a few others have emotional ties to certain hymns, prayers, or poems. But for the most part, this sort of thing is no longer alive. Most Christians of the space age do not conceive of the Christian life as one in which Jesus "walks with me, and . . . talks with me." Has anything taken the place of this Jesus piety? There does not seem to be any revived relationship with God through Jesus Christ. Vestiges of the Jesus cult may be present in the tendency to idealize Jesus as a hero embodying all the things we hold important: health, strength, beauty of face and body, a pleasant, outgoing personality. The crude version of this in a former generation would be Bruce Barton's *The Man Nobody Knows.* In our own generation, Hollywood made a direct pitch to this secular cult of Jesus, the human hero, in the motion picture *The King of Kings.* Naturally, a male star with tremendous sex appeal was chosen to play Jesus—Jeff Hunter. One critic had the following reaction when he saw the movie: "You'd know anywhere that this Jesus is a true American. Auburn hair and lovely blue eyes. The whole sequence reminded me of Billy Graham at Madison Square Garden".[10] Visual testimony to the presence of this hero cult are the thousands of sickeningly sentimental pictures of Jesus hanging in Protestant churches and homes. Many look like Rock Hudson with a beard. Their message is that we dare not think of Jesus as the despised and rejected Messiah with "no beauty that we should desire him" (Isa. 53:2). The hero cult takes Jesus as a human idol: strong, handsome, manly, a worthy object of our admiration. In short, he is taken as Jesus, but not as the Christ.

Yet we cannot feel too easy about leaving the whole matter at the point of these criticisms. Was there not a genuine intention and intuition behind Protestant piety's insistence that Jesus is in some way central to the Christian life? Is not Jesus Christ the real heart and soul of the whole "story" that has grasped and transformed every Christian? Is not the picture of the suffering disciple yet a valid one? Dare the Christian go at this matter of the Christian life without some reference to or relation to Jesus the Christ?

Chapter Three

THE PERILOUS WORLD OF
"CHRISTIAN PRINCIPLES"

> The meanest man I ever saw
> Allus kep' inside o' the law.
>
> —*James Whitcomb Riley*[11]

A third mark of Protestant piety sees the Christian life as life according to certain "Christian principles." Such principles reveal more specifically just how the Bible is our lamp and our guide, and how Jesus is our standard. The Bible and Jesus do not give us a detailed legal code, but they do provide us with some *principles* by which to live. Hence we describe a friend or acquaintance as a "man of principles." An act is a Christian act insofar as it expresses some Christian principle. Turning the other cheek, in a certain situation, would be necessary because that action applies the principle that we should respond to hostility and violence with nonhostility and nonviolence. The Christian life can be spelled out by a list of such principles. To live in accordance with them is to live the Christian life.

Furthermore, for our forefathers the content of such a list was fairly fixed and clear. A frequent way of organizing these Christian ideals is provided by the Ten Commandments, which thus are viewed as the ten principles of the Christian life. Another favorite summary of basic principles was the threefold sobriety, justice, and religion, which was actually a classification of the Ten Commandments. Various principles governed such spheres as eating, drinking, pleasures, thoughts, and relations to superiors such as elders, parents, or rulers. These spheres were regulated according to certain ideals such as temperance, modesty, chastity, and obedience. It was assumed that the existence of such principles would make clear, in most situations, the Christian act or attitude.

"Christian Principles in Exchange for . . ."

We must now ask, Is this the way contemporary Christians think of the Christian life? Do we run our lives according to a fixed list of fairly clear Christian principles or ideals? For instance, Protestant theologians have always spoken of certain "means of grace" (the proclaimed Word and the Sacraments), by which the Christian could progress in the Christian life. Is this what contemporary Christians are doing when they hear preaching and when they take the Sacraments? Are they gaining help and strength to enable them to live a "godly, righteous, and sober life?" I am not suggesting that Christians of the twentieth century have no "principles" at all. I am only wondering whether they look at the Christian life this way. I am also wondering whether the principles they do have are deliberately taken from the Christian gospel or from the Bible. Everyone of course has his pet hobby horse. A pushes missions; B stresses doing things as a family; and C sees all Christian virtues symbolized by total abstinence from alcoholic beverages. Yet the overall list of principles that members of a contemporary church take seriously is a kind of moral chef's salad which includes a few of the Ten Commandments, some customs recently sprouted in American suburbia, a little of the "American way of life," and a mishmash of advice from the *Reader's Digest* and the *Ladies' Home Journal*. It will do us no good to hide the matter. The "Christian principles" by which our grandfathers lived the Christian life are also gone with the wind.

What has replaced "Christian principles" in the space age? David Riesman has powerfully argued that the present generation of Americans does not look to the past for its values and standards. This being the case, the "Christian principles" of the Puritan and Victorian epochs can play no significant role. Rather, our generation looks carefully at its peer groups for the clues as to what is important or unimportant. Therefore, instead of principles derived from the Christian revelation, we live attuned to whatever is now in vogue. We still may call our standards Christian, but in our more honest moments we know we are stretching the word. For "Christian principles" now covers just about anything Americans, as a people, do and believe. Hence, we can, without a single wince or prick of conscience, use terms such as "Americanism," "patriotism," "capitalism," "nationalism," "democracy," "life on the patio," and "Christianity," as all standing for roughly the same thing. But regardless of our tricky vocabulary, the Christian principles of our grandfathers, like the grandfathers themselves, have now faded away.

Principles and the Word of God

Many theologians in the present generation are not particularly sad about the demise of the "principles" approach. A few questions may help illustrate the point.

1. What is the relation between the principle and the present will of the living God?

A principle is always a general summary or policy, not a specific dictate or command. As a general policy, the principle cannot itself be God's Word or will for a specific situation. It was Kierkegaard who drew the sharp line between ethical

principles and the contemporary speaking of the living God.[12]
If God's Word is identified with past principles to which we
resort when perplexed, then God is silent in the present. He
would be unable to speak a *present* Word to a novel situation.
There would be no Word of God for situations not covered by
the principles. Since principles cannot be specific, there
would be no Word of God for specific situations. The practical consequence of this is simply that God is dead. The present and the specific are cut off from him, for he is powerless
to penetrate into the present and the specific.

2. *What is the relation between the principle and the freedom
of man?*

Man, as he is portrayed in contemporary philosophy and
theology, is a strange kind of being. This "strangeness" is due
to the fact that the way man is truly himself, a human being,
is not determined for him in the same way a turnip is determined as a turnip. A turnip must be a turnip; a dog must be
a dog. A man can be a carpenter or politician, a worried or
confident being. Man, in a sense, is always determining what
he is, choosing what he is, in ways that go beyond mere in-
stinct. *Human* nature, therefore, is not merely a certain physi-
cal torso. Human nature must include this self-determination
of one's own nature.

Now, where do the principles fit into all of this? They perhaps serve to summarize certain insights as to what is good
and what is bad for man, physically, socially, and psychologically. But if God has made man as this self-determining being,
will a list of principles portray what man is to do and be? Even
"Christian principles"? Let us try to be more specific. All of
us constantly face novel situations. They may bear some re-
semblance to other situations, but they are never exact dupli-
cates. If man is a self-determining being, a choice confronts
him in each situation as to how he is to be himself in that situation. No principle can serve as that which determines. A

man may consult a principle, but even then he must still either interpret and apply it or reject it. This means that the principle itself is not what finally settles the matter. The situation of human decision is a very complicated situation which includes my own concrete and unique being with its concerns, habits, and drives, my self-determining act, the novel situation confronting me, the living Spirit of God, the content of revelation, principles and ideals, and who knows what else. For this reason, the Christian life can never be merely a matter of making decisions directly from fixed principles.

But we are not left with a very desirable situation. If "Christian principles" have been traded for a cultural potpourri, it seems as if the twentieth-century Christian has successfully isolated himself from any situation in which the Word of God might speak, as well as from the enduring wisdom of past civilizations and the Christian revelation. If that is the case, will not our victory celebrations about emancipation from our Victorian aunts and uncles have about them a rather forced and hysterical note?

Chapter Four

THE PIOUS PROVINCIALISM OF "RELIGIOUS DUTIES"

"Consider what your future will be like," he repeated. ". . . Drilling the Girl Guides, reading novels to the Mothers' Union, polishing the altar brasses, cadging money for the organ fund, making brown paper jackboots for the school-children's plays, keeping your end up in the vile little feuds and scandals of the church hen-coop. . . . You will sit through interminable church services which in the end will make you physically sick with their sameness and futility."

—*George Orwell*[13]

I tried to say in Chapter One that the Christian faith must express itself inevitably in concrete human attitudes and acts. The priority of God's grace makes it clear that we have no salvation in these acts themselves. The acts are consequences, fruits, attempts at obedient response to the saving God. In Protestant piety, however, religious acts take on a special function.

First of all, Protestant piety quite confidently listed *the* acts each Christian was obliged to perform or avoid. Hence, a definite and detailed pattern of necessary and forbidden acts described what it meant to be a Christian. Secondly, since these acts were necessary, they were the inevitable marks of the Christian. One could safely conclude that where such acts were absent, salvation was also absent. The acts themselves can serve as the rule, the set of standards, that tells us what to do and be. The Christian life then means performing these acts. Note that we are not talking about general principles, but about specific, usually observable acts.[14]

For centuries, Christian thinkers have divided the Ten Commandments into two types: duties in relation to man, and duties in relation to God. The duties toward God often serve as the basis for describing these necessary religious acts. One standard nineteenth-century analysis of the "religious duties" of the Christian lists the following external acts: (1) reading the Bible; (2) fasting; (3) keeping the religious festivals, especially the Sabbath; (4) prayer; (5) giving alms and doing works of charity; (6) repentance.

Compare the preceding list to that of a twentieth-century seminary professor:[15] (1) moral living, including breaking bad habits; (2) prayer and private worship; (3) uses of devotional literature including the Bible; (4) church attendance; (5) service to others, including witnessing and social action.

In some Protestant groups the list is longer and more detailed, including taboos such as drinking or cursing. In other groups the list is briefer. The point is that such lists designate what is "the Christian thing to do"—that which, if you are a Christian, you should do.

The Religious Parochialism of "Religious Acts"

One of the most striking matters about lists such as those above is the effect a *perspective* has on them. When we look at such a list as something with which we grew up, almost like the air we breathe, each item seems to be an absolutely unchangeable and indispensable expression of the Christian faith, each act something any Christian would unavoidably perform. When we place the list on a larger canvas of the history of Christendom, the items begin to look very parochial.

Some ages and Christian groups looked at the Christian life as involving essentially only one set of acts, partaking of the Sacraments of the church. In such a sacramental piety, the Christian life means regular going to confession, which is a preparation for attending Mass. There are, of course, virtues to be developed and sins avoided (or confessed). But these may characterize the pagan world. What makes a Christian a Christian is this pattern of confession and Eucharist.

Another branch of Christendom, oriented to the phenomenon of conversion, sees the Christian life as a life of soul-winning, attending revivals, being reconverted and rededicated. Still another age and time sees the Christian life as one of solitary contemplation of God. In some patterns, Bible-reading has no place at all. In several patterns, church attendance is important, but for quite different reasons, for instance, the Roman Catholics, the Lutherans, and the Quakers. Even more variety occurs when we consider the absolutely forbidden taboos listed by Christian groups. For example, the majority of Christians in the world do not observe the Mohammedan taboo of absolute abstinence from alcohol.

Such relativity of "religious acts" forces us then to raise a question. Is the pattern of religious duties in Protestant piety necessary, able thus to describe what any Christian will unavoidably do? At this point, we must either stick with religious parochialism to its bitter end, insisting that the only Christians around are those following the five (or four, or six, or one hundred and eighty-seven) duties of Protestant piety, or we replace "necessary" with "likely," "possible," or "silly." It is one thing to point out that, when possible, Christians will spontaneously form a gathering in which they pursue their common aims. It is quite another thing to say that God's saving forgiveness will inevitably and always result in acts A, B, and C.

An example might be that of membership in some contemporary denomination and the associated activities of church work, church attendance, and church contributions. Is it conceivable that a Christian might be a Christian outside such a pattern? Before answering too quickly, we should be conscious of a growing body of "churchless Christians" (should we call them "underground Christians"?) whose disillusionment with the contemporary church institution makes it imperative for them to stay out. In such cases, nonchurchmanship is not an expression of their apathy but of their faith. We may well answer that the church would be better off with their presence and their criticism. Therefore they have no right to remain outside the walls of the institution. Such an argument could be right in some rationalistic sense. But at least the existence of such Christians is conceivable. And in the larger plan the existence of such a group may be desirable, even a response to the call and Word of God. *Not only is it conceivable.* For many years Japanese Christendom has seen just such a phenomenon in the *Mukyōkai,* or Non-Church movement. Ten years ago, these people, attempting to be Christians outside the institutional church, numbered at least fifty thousand. This is not to say they are right. But then, do we know they are wrong? Likewise, conceivable is a Christian who does not read his Bible regularly. The point is that the concrete way faith expresses itself over the world does not correspond exactly with Protestant piety's list of duties and taboos.

The Neighborhood Parochialism of Religious Activities

However we argue about what *ought* to be, we must now live with a new fact. Along with other aspects of Protestant piety, necessary religious acts and essential duties of the Christian are going with the wind. How many contemporary church members see, as essential and necessary expressions of their faith, regular Bible study, prayer, the worship of God, repentance, and the rest? Some church members may take up some of these acts, but the total structure or pattern is gone.

In its place we have religious *activities*, or better, church activities. The contemporary church member probably spends more time in and about the church than his pious forefathers. In connection with the church, he sits on committees, repairs, paints, plays cards, goes on camping trips, serves as adviser, gives money, cooks, teaches, skates, discusses, hears sermons, bowls, eats, etc., etc., etc.—all done in what now remains, along with the country club, the most segregated and socially stratified institution in America. In place of religious duties, church activities now provide the essential marks of the Christian, the standards of the Christian life, and the clues as to "the Christian thing to do." To what end is all the bustle? Unlike the religious acts of Protestant piety, it does not seem to be for edification, nor, for that matter, for any religious purpose at all. Such church activity appears to be less a religious act (a response to God's grace), and more an extension of what it means to be a responsible member of a neighborhood. Insofar as such activities do have a religious prompting at all, it seems to be due to a combination of the vacuum left by the vanishing of traditional patterns of piety and of the remaining desire to "be religious" and a serious Christian. Churchy busyness may not seem to be much, but for many that is all that is left.

Chapter Five

THE CORRUPTIBILITY OF
"RELIGIOUS EXPERIENCE"

We shall not go to a room at 8 o'clock and proceed to find God,
if by finding God you mean feeling "Sunday-nightish" or what
some of my friends call "bubbly."

—*Leslie Weatherhead*[16]

And I also knew by now, alas, far more about divine inspiration than I dared admit, for I knew how I worked myself up
into my own visions, and how frequently—indeed, incessantly
—the visions God granted to me differed from the visions He
granted to my father.

—*James Baldwin*[17]

According to Jonathan Edwards, the great American Puritan
theologian and perhaps *the* American theologian to date,
"As true religion is of a practical nature, and God hath so
constituted the human nature that the affections are very
much the spring of men's actions, this also shows that true
religion must consist very much in the affections."[18] By *affections,* Edward meant the will and the emotions of man, symbolized as things of the "heart." We should not be surprised
that the Christian faith, being what it is, finds expression in
the emotive or feeling aspects of human nature. Words like
"sin," "repentance," "forgiveness," and "worship" do not
stand merely for intellectual theories. The Christian knows
what these things are by sinning, repenting, worshiping, and

being forgiven. Nor are these activities merely intellectual or mental processes. Repenting is not a cold-blooded and calcuative decision to turn from sin to God. Because sin itself is a personal act involving scorn for God and hurt for other men, repentance too is a personal act, including with it such things as fear, regret, and resolve. "Religious affections" then, are inevitable and legitimate expressions of faith.

Nor should we be surprised to hear that some periods in the history of Christendom stressed religious feeling more than other periods. In the early centuries of the Christian era, Montanism was just such a movement. In the Middle Ages various types of mysticism "practiced the presence of God." In Reformation times the so-called left wing of the Reformation, the Anabaptist groups, gave fiery and agitated expression to the faith. Emphasis on the Christian life as a life marked by deep and sometimes dramatic emotional experiences became a standard part of Protestant piety about the end of the seventeenth century in German Pietism, in Puritanism, and in the Methodist movement led by the Wesleys. The Great Awakening of frontier days, the various waves of revivalism, including the recent Billy Graham crusades, the continued presence and growth of Pentecostal-type groups, and the liberal theologies of "religious experience" have all helped American Protestant piety retain this element as one of its chief marks.

Is Repentance a Feeling?

The phenomenon is not necessarily one about which we can be completely happy. The emotions of human nature are full of tricks and traps, and the same holds for religious emotions. Stress on emotions is an easily corrupted thing, and this is just what happened in Protestant piety.

The first step in the corruption of religious emotions occurs when the *basic realities testified to in the proclamation of the* gospel are identified with certain feelings and experiences. Guilt thereby becomes then merely a *feeling* of guilt; God's forgiveness exists only insofar as I *feel* forgiven; worship means certain experiences and feelings in a certain setting. Two matters are omitted in such identifications. One is that such realities as guilt and forgiveness have their basis in God himself. If guilt is established "in the eyes of God," if sin is against God, if forgiveness is at the hands of God, then these words stand for something more than just our feelings or emotions that arise in connection with these realities. Secondly, such identifications omit the role our minds play in the matter. Forgiveness is not merely mediated in a feeling. Forgiveness is received in connection with a proclaimed gospel, and has something to do with Jesus Christ. Therefore, our experience of forgiveness or worship includes an interpretation on our part, a grasping with the mind of certain claims. If such realities are merely emotions, this implies that sin, forgiveness, and the rest can be grasped apart from the good news of Jesus Christ.

Tears That Tell and Sighs That Waft

The second step in the corruption of religious emotions in Protestant piety occurs when *the emotions become the final goal of the Christian life.* When this happens, the emotions become the tests of whether or not we are living the Christian life. Note the subtle change that has taken place. In worship the goal is no longer to worship God, but to experience a worshipful feeling. In salvation our striving is not to receive God's pardon, but to have a feeling that will enable us to rest easily and not worry about our relation to God.

The hymnody of Protestant piety is painful testimony to this very thing. In the period when hymns were still primarily paraphrases of psalms, the hymn functioned as the expression of faith in God, of worship of God. If they were celebrations,

they celebrated the great events of salvation and God's part
in them. For instance, the familiar sixteenth-century hymn
based on Psalm 100:

> All people that on earth do dwell,
>   Sing to the Lord with cheerful voice;
> Him serve with mirth, his praise forthtell,
>   Come ye before him and rejoice.

Emotion is present here (cheer, mirth, rejoicing), but it is
clearly not for its own sake. Its purpose is the praise of God.
Contrast this to Wesley's description of salvation. I should
clarify that I am not citing this hymn as typical or representa-
tive of Wesley; rather, it serves to illustrate the basic switch
in piety when emotions themselves are pursued as goals.

> A pardon written with his blood,
> The favor and the peace of God;
> The *seeing eye,* the *feeling sense,*
> The mystic *joys* of penitence;
> The godly *fear,* the *pleasing smart,*
> The *meltings* of a broken heart;
> The *tears* that tell your sins forgiven;
> The *sighs* that waft your souls to heaven.[19]

How is it that tears tell us our sins are forgiven? How do sighs
waft us to heaven? We have here an almost pure example of
how feelings themselves can become the criteria and therefore
the goal of the Christian life. Yet we must admit that feelings
come rather cheap. A few psychological and aesthetic gimmicks will whip them up. Even apart from such gimmicks,
tears and sighs can be self-induced. We will give special attention to inducing them if we suspect that they will waft us to
heaven, or make us Christians. How, then, dare we identify
such tricky psychological entities with the presence of God,
the Word of God, the salvation of God, or the realities of God?
Furthermore, when religious feelings are an end in themselves, all the events and realities of our relation with God are

measured by the presence of such feelings. Conversion is real only if it comes in an identifiable experience. A minister knows he has "the call" only by the presence of certain kinds of emotion. A service of worship is "successful" only when certain feelings are produced. Prayer really is prayer and not just saying words only when accompanied by a tear or a sigh. Now we must ask very bluntly, How do we know this? How dare we say to the Spirit of God that he is unable to speak through ordinary events and processes: through the reflection of our minds, through a situation that presents itself? How dare we assume that our emotions and our need for emotions are immune from sin and pride? Surely we do assume this when we claim that God is automatically present *whenever* certain feelings are present.

"Lord, Give Us All a Nice Feeling This Morning"

The third and final step in which religious emotions are corrupted in Protestant piety proceeds quite expectedly from the first two steps. If "my feelings" and "my experiences" are the goal of the Christian life, then the real object of my concern is not God but myself. Once that step is taken and "my feelings" are made central, the next expected step is to censor and sift the emotions, letting in only those in which "I" find some comfort and consolation. This restricts the way in which God is present to me. Since the feelings are for the sake of myself and my enjoyment, all threatening modes of God's presence are abolished. The feelings of the Christian life are limited to peace, companionship, consolation, and rest, thus excluding any possibility that God is present to me as judge, corrector, and a troubler of the waters. This means that real repentance and real forgiveness are eliminated.

Bishop Christopher Wordsworth observed this very process in the growth of Protestant hymnody. "The pronouns *I* and *my*," he says, "are rarely found in any ancient Church hymn. But in modern hymns the individual often detaches and isolates himself from the body of the faithful; and in a spirit of sentimental selfishness obtrudes his own feelings concerning himself."[20] This leads directly to the filling-station theory of Sunday morning worship. Worn out and empty from the futilities and discouragements of the week, we attend weekly worship to get the batteries recharged and the tank refilled. Even as these words are being written, a major American denomination is pushing a piece of advertising over nationwide television crudely suggesting that going to church each Sunday is for the purpose of getting one's "spiritual" batteries recharged. This is in the same line, and almost as crude, as the radio commercials now being pushed by the Presbyterians. One of them implies that we should go to church regularly so we won't lose certain "blessings" and so we won't get caught out on a limb. So the lines between Yahwism and Baalism are again drawn, between the God who expects his people to serve *him* and the god who is expected to serve (bless, charge up the batteries, etc.) the *people*.

Some sociologists are now saying that this is the basic way the modern suburban church functions in our culture. The suburbanite's world is a twofold one: the city (where he works) and the suburb (where he spends his leisure). The church is not only *in* the suburb geographically; its function is identified with the function of the suburb, namely, as the retreat, the haven, a part of the leisure world where we go to rest and to be consoled before returning to work.[21] Insofar as this is the case, the following hymn could serve as a motto for the consolation-oriented Christian.

> There is a place of quiet rest,
> A place where sin cannot molest,
> There is a place of comfort sweet,
> A place where we our Saviour meet,
> There is a place of full release,
> A place where all is joy and peace,
> Near to the heart of God.[22]

David Head has satirized the filling-station Christian in a delightful collection of "prayers for the natural man." Here is one of them:

> Lord, give us all a nice feeling this morning. We pray that we may enjoy the preliminaries, and that the sermon may give us all a glow. I know I have offended at least two people this week with my quick temper, but please do not let the thought of that intrude upon this spiritual feast.[23]

So Protestant piety has run its course from the legitimate recognition of "religious affections" to the motif of retreat into the self and its feelings, isolated thus from the sufferings of the neighbor and from the terrifying objectivity of the Word of God.

A Space-Age Substitute

But the twentieth-century Christian has moved beyond even Protestant piety and its corruption of religious feelings. A vestige of *feelings* remains, but the basic exchange has been made, for space-age Christians have traded *religious* emotions for churchly and aesthetic emotions. As feelings, they do not accompany the realities of the gospel. They do not occur in conjunction with guilt, repentance, forgiveness, or worship. Hence they appear not to be religious feelings at all, for the situation in which they arise is aesthetic—the effects of church architecture, the oratorical gimmicks of the preacher, the sunset at the church camp, the dramatic anthem of the choir.

Dare we raise a timid question about that Sunday morning Sacred Cow, the anthem? I have a musician friend who was made the object of bitter insult and vilification (and who, at one point, thought he would be physically attacked) for mildly raising this question in a group of church organists and choir directors. For what purpose is this climactic and aesthetically polished musical event in the middle of a period of worship? It does not proclaim the Word of God. The congregation itself expresses nothing by it, since at this point it is merely an audience. It is not a *background* of worship, pointing to something else, since as a performance it calls attention only to itself. Obviously it produces aesthetic emotions, as music is wont to do. But this is a reason against, not for, its inclusion in a service of worship. The performance orientation of the anthem prevents it from being a mere means to worship. But it is understandable why there is violent resistance to any suggestion that the anthem be eliminated. Since genuine religious affections are now replaced by aesthetically produced feelings, morning worship without the anthem might mean no feelings at all. And when religion and aesthetic feeling are identified, this means no religion at all. Eliminating the anthem would be like eliminating God from the service. No wonder my friend was almost murdered for his mild suggestion.

Like the other marks of Protestant piety, we can be of two minds when we reflect on the religious emotions and their exchange. We are prone to cheer over the collapse of the corrupted emphasis on religious emotions with its psychological naïveté and its religious idolatry. But who can be happy about the substitute?

sinlier perfection

THE TERRIBLE CRIME OF
A "GUILTLESS ACT"

The persisting American illusion that there can be an escape
from politics had received a blow. Perhaps it was about to die,
but it would be a painful death.

—*William Miller*[24]

The church does not seem to realize how unethical a conven-
tionally respectable life may be.

—*Reinhold Niebuhr*[25]

With the exception of traditional Methodism and other
similar groups, Protestantism, by and large, has agreed that
Christian perfection is not a possibility, at least this side of
the resurrection. Yet Protestant piety, especially as it crystal-
lized in the Victorian era, did commit itself to something that
looks like perfectionism. Saying this is easier than clarifying
it. I shall make the attempt by asking a difficult question.
What is the *unit* of obedience in the Christian life? I mean by
that, what is it in the Christian life that is good or bad, right
or wrong, righteous or sinful, to be praised or to be condemned? The question itself smacks of perfectionism. Do
obedience or disobedience, good or evil, and all the rest fall
into clearly distinguishable units? Apparently, in Protestant
piety they do. Victorian piety knew very clearly that there
were good men and evil men. The distinction was clear be-

cause doing and thinking good things was easily distinguishable from doing and thinking evil things.

Clifton Olmstead portrays the Victorian Protestant as concerned mainly about a "reputation for piety, charity, and
unimpeachable conduct."[26] But we can speak meaningfully
about unimpeachable conduct only if good and evil reside in
conscious, obvious, and controllable units such as acts (including negative acts like resisting a temptation), thoughts,
and spoken words, all of which make up a person's conduct,
his character, and his reputation. The Victorian storekeeper
could be quite content with himself if he could say he never
once knowingly cheated a customer. The Victorian housewife
could feel beyond human and divine reproach if she re-
mained faithful to her husband in deed and thought and
always gave him his "satisfaction." That sin and guilt might
reach deeper than overt thoughts and actions never seemed
to occur to those caught up in this strand of Protestant piety.

Puritan piety expressed a similar notion in its great emphasis upon *self-examination* as a regular discipline in the
Christian life. Self-examination called for a daily inquiry into
one's motives, feelings, and conduct. The godly and devout
life itself was a matter of "escaping or mortifying sins" (un-
belief, hardness of heart, hypocrisy), "performing duties," and
"overcoming temptations." Sins, duties, virtues, and good
deeds were the terms enabling Christians to think about and
practice the Christian life. Furthermore, the sins and duties
could be listed. Certain acts and thoughts were always evil
and to be shunned. Other acts and thoughts were always good
and to be pursued. Such a simple picture of the human being
does not explicitly claim perfection, but it implies its possibility.

Personal Purity Versus Social Responsibility

Now we must ask, Is the unit of the Christian life the act
or thought that can be purely good or purely evil? Actions

always occur in a situation that includes other events, actions, and their consequences, all working together to produce a new situation. Even a simple action on our part can have consequences that hurt and destroy some parties in the situation. Politics is perhaps the clearest example. An effort to get through a governmental body a bill that is desperately needed by the people may not be possible apart from under-the-table agreements, "deals," compromises with opponents, perhaps even voting for something else that is against one's principles. Getting that bill through, or any bill through, may require working with and staying quiet about a criminal element, caucusing against friends, and, on several issues, disappointing the people whom one is supposed to support. Given the nature of power and the complex interdependence of events, the alternative is either to play these games or to retire from the scene. Such a retreat would mean that those who are tough enough and hard enough to work in power structures merely take over. It also means, in all probability, that the badly needed bill does not make it. The person who does retreat may retain some sort of "personal purity" by not being involved in any compromises. He is at the same time politically ineffective so that his "principles" and good causes are now turned over to his enemies who have no qualms or hesitations about the use of power. If his logic were carried out all the way, no "good" man would ever be part of politics at all.

Furthermore, it is the Victorian mind-set that repudiates politics as "dirty," and thinks that by staying out of Washington, the state capital, or the city council, a person's purity can be retained. Now we must say quite bluntly that this assumption that "politics" (and therefore compromise, etc.) is merely a matter of governmental situations having nothing to do with ordinary "pure" life is a figment of the Victorian imagination. "Politics" occurs wherever human groups plan and decide effectively. And each individual's everyday decisions are made as responses to the actions of various power groups. According to Gayraud S. Wilmore:

The decisions that a man makes about where he will live, how he will furnish his home (the women's magazines, of course, will make this decision in co-operation with the furniture manufacturers), how he will discipline his children, what radio and TV commentators he will listen to, what newspapers and magazines he will subscribe to, and what organizations he will join in his community—all of these daily decisions are, to an inestimable but unquestionable degree, influenced by the legislation, education, and plain ballyhoo daily propagated by these groups and the power centers that control them.[27]

Almost every situation that confronts us is potentially political: the children in a family hatching some scheme to spring on the father, the various struggles in a sales organization, the administration of a church organization. Because of the interplay and competition of the interests of different groups and persons, life itself, in the family and in society, is a matter of continual balance and adjustment. Absolute personal purity can be attained only to the degree that the person retreats from the competition and adjustments of life in society. Thus the choice that Victorian piety insists on is between personal purity (sticking exactly to the taboos and the duties) and social responsibility. Victorian piety, in other words, is the Protestant version of the Catholic monastic ideal. But what sort of morality and purity is it that is purchased at the expense of tyranny, poverty, economic oppression by a small group, the dictatorship of labor or management, or racial segregation which eats up the souls of both Negro and white alike? "Personal purity" at those prices puts forth a very foul odor.

Personal Purity Versus the Word of God

Actually, the same criticism holds here that was leveled at other marks of Protestant piety. Something other than the Word of God is determining the Christian life. The Victorian moralist is trying to be sinless, which means he is concerned not with God's living Word but with a fixed and static ideal. For instance, Joe Smith feels strongly that Christians must obey all civil laws, and that to break such laws is sinful. Now it is conceivable that God calls this Joe Smith to participation in the racial revolution, which will involve tacit approval of or even participation in civil disobedience. Joe Smith rejects this call and remains "sinless" and "pure." But he has rejected the Word of God addressed to him. What he has actually done is to claim that God's Word is synonymous with a fixed list of taboos and duties. Any participation in society's problems that involves a break with those taboos or a lapse of those duties is ruled out. God is able thus to say nothing in the present that is not on the list of taboos or duties. God therefore, for all practical purposes, is dead. Instead of God, the Victorian moralist has his codes which he absolutizes, worships, and obeys. We can only conclude then that the pursuit of a perfect and guiltless act is a terrible crime against God as well as against man.

The Victorian ideal of personal purity, with its absolutely righteous acts and thoughts, is still present in our age, but in a very different way from that of a generation ago. The twentieth-century Christian does not worry very much about the purity of his every act or thought. He intuitively recognizes that Aunt Sarah thinks and talks that way, but such talk is only the residue of another age. There are, of course, matters in which a general consensus still obtains about rightness or wrongness. But the goal of attaining righteousness through the purity of every act or thought, "unimpeachable conduct," is fast moving from the scene.

In spite of this we still have emotional ties to the Victorian moral universe and the clichés that express it. One symptom of this was the "morality" issue of the 1964 presidential campaign. The controversy and the propaganda were strictly Victorian. "Morality" did not mean the capacity or willingness of the candidates to pursue the best welfare for the total country. It meant "unimpeachable conduct," purity in thought and act with no compromises, no deals. Now most politicians know that morality in the former sense is a real responsibility and in the latter sense is a fake. But they also recognize that the residue in America of an emotional attachment to the moral clichés of the Victorian era is an important mind-set to be appealed to in political propaganda and for campaign issues. My own suspicion goes somewhat farther. Because we do intuitively sense that the old "personal purity" way of thinking is really gone, and gone even within ourselves, we almost hysterically cling to the symbols and phrases of our past, and vehemently resist (at the level of words and feelings) any symptoms of the change. What we do not do is order our own lives and thoughts according to the perfectionist ideal of personal purity.

Personal purity being present today merely as an emotional attachment to an ideal from a former time, has anything taken its place? Is there a contemporary substitute for the Victorian ideal of guiltless acts and thoughts? The following suggestion admittedly is a speculation. Even as a speculation, it may hold as yet for a rather small circle. One of the most repeated themes in theology in recent decades is the Pauline and Reformation "justification by faith," God's gracious forgiveness rather than one's meritorious works. This is the order of the day. Justification may well be the central doctrine of Christian theology. It surely is one of the most dangerous. "God forgives everything I do," can very quickly become a cover-up for an easy conscience. The temptation is to see the Christian life as something without demand, without law, without rigorous discipline, and without warfare and struggle. The end result is to see ourselves automatically on chummy terms with God because there is really nothing (law, demand, sin, idolatry) about which God could be angry. Some readers will recognize in this the now familiar distinction of Dietrich Bonhoeffer between cheap and costly grace. He describes cheap grace as follows:

Rom. 5 Shall we sin that grace may abound

The world has been justified by grace. The Christian knows that, and takes it seriously. He knows he must not strive against this indispensable grace. Therefore—let him live like the rest of the world! . . . Let him be comforted and rest assured in his possession of this grace—for grace alone does everything. Instead of following Christ, let the Christian enjoy the consolations of his grace! That is what we mean by cheap grace. . . . Cheap grace is the preaching of forgiveness without requiring repentance, baptism without church discipline, Communion without confession, absolution without personal confession. Cheap grace is grace without discipleship, grace without the cross, grace without Jesus Christ, living and incarnate.[28]

Cheap grace and cheap forgiveness call to mind an incident in the lives of Walt Kelly's Pogo and his friends. Several of the irrepressible little animals exuberantly "forgive" one of their friends. "We forgives you. We forgives you," they cry. The response is classic. "How would you like a punch in the nose?" Victorian "personal purity" seems now to be exchanged for sentimental attachment to the Victorian phrases and for cheap grace. If these represent the choice before us, what a terrible either-or!

Chapter Seven

THE FAKE WORLD OF
GUILTLESS MOTIVES

You ask what makes me sigh, old friend,
What makes me shudder so?
I shudder and I sigh to think
That even Cicero
And many-minded Homer were
Mad as the mist and snow.

—William Butler Yeats[29]

One mark of Protestant piety is the rather naïve portrayal of good and evil as occurring in obvious and controllable units such as acts and thoughts. These acts and thoughts can be either pure or not pure, good or bad. The previous chapter accused this view of ignoring the complexities of social and political responsibilities. Protestant piety, however, goes farther in its case for purity. It reaches down to our very motivations and insists that these should also be guiltless. How often have we heard about people who have "unchristian motives" for church attendance, who are in church only for social reasons? How often have we heard how a certain action is suspect because it expresses a sinful or selfish motive? A certain moralistic sociology today has apparently inherited this piety of pure motivation. According to this literature, people who buy better houses, move up the social ladder, buy

Buicks instead of Chevrolets, attend the Presbyterian or Episcopal churches instead of the Church of God, are all motivated by selfish, social-climbing devices and are to be pitied or condemned.

This piety of pure motives falls short on three counts: the frequent irrelevance of the motivational element in the ethical situation, the collapse of the myth of "pure" motives under the probing of depth psychology, and the inadequate understanding of the self. I will discuss the first two now, saving the third for Chapter Ten.

The Irrelevance of Pure Motives

An ethical situation is a situation that calls for some kind of response or decision. Ethical situations vary tremendously in their importance and urgency. Voting for a Presidential candidate is an ethical situation. So is the racial revolution, and so is a bad highway accident that calls for immediate help. We can see already how irrelevant it would be to make "pure motivation" the condition of responding to such situations. When people are bleeding and dying in a highway accident, the situation demands help regardless of the motives of the helper. The one immoral response to that situation would be to stop and engage in a long self-analysis to find out whether one's motives for helping are sound. One man may help because the state law says he must; another, because he could not live with his guilty conscience if he did not help; another, because he hopes to get some publicity out of the incident. If you and I were faced with such a situation, and we did find that our basic motivation was publicity-seeking, would this justify not helping? Of course not. Whatever the motives, the situation itself calls for help. If I did engage in internal self-analysis in the face of such a situation, it would imply that I, with my purity, was the only thing in the whole world that counted.

The characters in the "sick" world of Jules Feiffer[30] are pitiful examples of this sort of thing. They appear to be very sophisticated, but they carry the Victorian logic of purity of motivation out to the bitter end. They *appear* to talk to other human beings and respond to situations outside themselves. But let us not be fooled. The whole world is merely a projection of themselves, a stage on which they carry on a sickly and paralyzing monologue with themselves. Ironically, the constant worry about whether motives are selfish or not puts the self right on stage center and turns out to be the sickest form of the idolatry of the self.

A brief clarification: I am not saying that motivations cannot be distinguished or that they make no difference at all. Obviously, helping out in a highway accident out of compassion for the suffering is more appropriate to the situation than a vulturelike assistance on the prowl for publicity. However, this problem is bound up with the total problem of that human being and his redemption. As such it must be dealt with over the long term. In the meantime, the ethical situations themselves must guide our responses, whatever our motivations.

The Motives Behind the Motives

Now we must pursue the fundamental problem. *Are* there pure motives? In more theological language, are there guiltless and sinless motives, motives that are not in any way expressions of idolatrous pride and deep-rooted impulses to hurt, manipulate, and destroy? Traditional Protestant piety could give an easy affirmative to this question. Remember, Protestant piety saw the bearer of good and evil to be a controllable and conscious unit such as an act or thought. The same holds for the motive. The motive is a conscious and controllable thing. It is also a transparent thing. If my motive for working for promotion is, let us say, to give my family certain necessities and luxuries, then the matter is ended. The motive is simply whatever I am conscious of and will acknowledge.

Fortunately, this simple Victorian world of simple and translucent motives is now gone. The discovery of the sub-conscious dimension of human personality has eliminated the Victorian "pure motive." Motive in the sense of a conscious intention, purpose, or reason for acting is never wholly iso-lated from a subconscious background. The distinction itself is clearly manifested when we realize the difference between the content of our dreams or what comes forth under narco-synthesis and the usual thoughts and "motives" that make up our consciousness. Residing deeply in the being of every hu-man are impulses, needs, fears, and lusts which, when ex-pressed, are more appropriate to a jungle than a Victorian parlor. The subconscious dimension is, of course, not merely evil. But it does show that our conscious motives are not the whole picture. The motivation for our acts reaches deeply into the subconscious world for its roots and origins. Because of this I cannot be so sure that my only motive for working for promotion is simply to help my family. That may be merely my rational disguising of my hostility toward a cer-tain person and my struggle to displace him, or my struggle to gain power in the corporation, or my compulsive desire to order and subdue the world around me. Therefore, I can never be sure that the motives I admit to are free from idolatrous pride and deep-rooted impulses to conquer, de-stroy, assert, or possess.

William Golding's novel *Lord of the Flies* is a frightening portrayal of how thinly civilized impulses are painted on the jungle impulse of human nature. The story depicts a group of boys shipwrecked and alone on a remote desert island, without guidance or restraint. The stripping off of the veneer of civilization takes only a few days. The boys not only be-come animal hunters, fascinated with the act of killing and the symbol of blood. They begin to hunt each other. And the impulses to track and kill and eat are all bound up with primitive sexual impulses. When the rescuing boat arrives, civilization is again painted on and they become proper English gentlemen.

Protestantism should not have needed the advent of Freudian analysis to puncture the myth of pure motives. From Biblical times on, this same insight has been present in the literature of Christian theology. Augustine, Pascal, Luther, Edwards, Kierkegaard—all portrayed man the sinner in ways that retained the corrupted world of the depths.

Actually, both Freudian and theological criticisms are now beside the point. Twentieth-century Christians are quite unlike their Victorian grandfathers in these respects. Whatever twentieth-century Christians *are* up to, they are not worrying very much whether or not their motives are pure. An important part of the Christian life as the Puritans conceived it was "self-examination." Special attention was given to examining one's deepest motives and intentions. Apparently, the only kind of psychological or mental discipline today's Christians are taking up are techniques for gaining personal confidence, peace of mind, or freedom from worry. Instead of worrying about guilty motives, our "self-analysis," when done at all, is designed to eliminate all worrying. Here too, we live in a very different kind of moral and religious universe from that of our forefathers.

Chapter Eight

On clop

THE PAGAN PIETY
OF "CHRISTIAN VIRTUES"

"I think God has given us the love of special places,
  of a hearth and of a native land, for a good reason." ∟
"I dare say," I said, "What reason?"
"Because otherwise," he said, pointing his pole out at
  the sky and the abyss,
"We might worship that."
"What do you mean?" I demanded.
"Eternity," he said in his harsh voice,   *Immitatity*
"the largest of the idols—the mightiest of the
  rivals of God."

              —*G. K. Chesterton*[31]

Protestant piety's concern with Christian virtues, Christian
character, and personal purity goes beyond acts and motives.
Protestant piety inherited from Catholic piety the fear of
worldliness and the scorn of the body and the self. The devotional literature of Protestant piety is filled with such
phrases as "worldly pleasures," "temptations of the flesh,"
and "surrendering one's will to God." These phrases find
their origins in the Scriptures. Paul constantly contrasted flesh
and Spirit (e.g., Rom., ch. 8); the Fourth Gospel speaks of the
world that hates the Christ. The disciples represent a kingdom not of the world. The disciples are also told to deny
themselves and follow Christ.

However, it would be quite erroneous to conclude from such passages that the world, the flesh, the self, and the human will are simply evil in contrast to heaven, the soul, and the will of God. The "world" that rejects Christ stands for a creation of God ruled temporarily by other powers than God. Yet God sends the Messiah into this world, and the sphere of his coming Kingdom is nothing else but this world. Paul's contrast of flesh and Spirit focuses upon man in the weakness of his nature and caught in sin, thereby unable to save himself. Flesh in this sense is not body, but embraces personal and "spiritual" aspects of man. Hence, the "sins of the flesh" are envy, malice, and the like. "Denying oneself" to follow Christ must be seen in the light of man's total situation, in which the self makes itself into God and declares war on God. Denying this self would not mean, however, an attempt to annihilate the personal, willing, "self" aspect of man.

Protestant *theology* has always recognized such meanings.[32] The corruption, however, took place in Protestant *piety*. One way of describing this distorted interpretation of the Christian life is to compare it to an ancient (and some say modern) heresy called *docetism*. Docetism was simply the refusal to acknowledge that Jesus Christ was really and fully a human being. The reason behind this refusal was that the world, the flesh, the body, were in themselves evil, and God therefore could never "assume flesh." Note this distinction. It is one thing to describe the world, the flesh, and the self as weak, incapable of self-salvation, or corrupted by sin. One can still say that these are God's creations, and God is capable of restoring them to their intended status. It is quite another matter to describe them as purely evil, implying that God created an evil thing and that salvation must always be an escape from these spheres rather than a reconstruction of them. It was this latter view which insinuated itself among the themes and strands of Protestant piety, more a mood or a tone than an explicit doctrine. Protestant piety could thus conceive of personal purity in terms of individual virtues, selflessness, and spirituality. In this present chapter we shall look at Protestant piety's attitude toward the world, and in Chapter Ten, its attitude toward the self.

The Piety of My Comfort, My Virtues, and My Holiness

What is "the world"? As I am using the term, "world" stands for the totality of created things, persons, relations, and events *in* which any of us finds himself. It includes the various situations that appear before us to which we must respond. Since these situations vary from person to person, "my" world is not identical with "your" world. The world, therefore, stands for all created things, the cosmos, and the particular piece of all this which impinges on a person. In other words, the world includes the East and the West, America, various social crises, and various immediate environments, such as the place of work, and home, and the place in which recreation and leisure are pursued.

Now, the mood of Protestant piety toward the world in the above sense is a *docetic* mood; that is, a mood that emphasizes the unreality or unimportance, or even the evil, of the world. This mood prompts a retreat from the world to "a place of quiet rest near to the heart of God." Such a mood is qualified in some respects in Protestant piety. The missionary thrust to tell the story in all lands shows an awareness of the world. So does the Puritan emphasis on justice and a man being responsible in his civil duties.

But what evidence is there for the mood of world denial? The basic evidence is the fact that Protestant piety sees the Christian life mostly in terms of attaining and maintaining *individual* virtues. The great bulk of Protestant hymns pertaining to the Christian life is aimed at individual goals and wishes: *my* relation to Jesus, *my* temptations, *my* comfort in the face of life's trials, *my* holiness and godliness, *my* virtues of patience, trust, faith, contentment, purity, etc. Protestant piety is very similar to that kind of Catholic piety which centers about *my* sins and their absolution, *my* safety (thus St. Christopher figures in the car), and *my* saintliness. Protestants do not have a formal doctrine of "saints" in the sense of outstanding Christians and martyrs canonized by the church. Yet it would be fair to say that the saint is the basic goal of Protestant piety. For the goal of pious activities such as praying, Bible-reading, and corporate worship is one's *own* saintliness or godliness. Therefore, *Advice to a Young Christian* could say that the real business of life is our devout duties that further the good of the soul. Hence, "social obligations, and the relative duties of life . . . are not of first importance."

The Piety of World Denial

A second evidence for the mood of world denial is the frequent contrast between this life and the next, and the attempt to locate all meaning and importance in the next life. The contrast is between earth and heaven, darkness and glory, struggle and triumph, waiting and arrival. Such talk not only sounds more like Hinduism than the Old and New Testaments; it also makes one wonder why God bothered to create the world at all. How different is the mood of the letter mailed last year from India by an American teacher and artist. He anticipates a furlough to America, and he records the hundreds of things he is going to miss about India that he has grown to love and enjoy:

> The hundred spring shades of green on the hill, our ducks Soda and Rye (quackers), our grey tiger cat with his yellow eyes and his cocker spaniel size and his "What-do-you-want-Peasant?" manner, crows singing fugues in the warm blue air, rhododendrons like trees blossoming with rubies, the Himalayan thrush singing long cryptic sentences (like the one in *The Hobbit*), a little bird that shoots through the leafage like a chip of turquoise skipped along waves of emerald, camels

and buffalos of the Punjab. . . . Luckily we're Christians and don't need to feel guilty about getting so much pleasure out of material things and human beings; the Bible teaches that God made earth as well as heaven, flesh as well as spirit, and that Our Lord has redeemed them all.[33]

Christian Virtues Versus the Word of God

Christian worldliness, however, is more than the deep-seated and joyful response to God's creation. The issue is a very sharp one. We must make up our minds between "saintliness" with its virtues and life according to the Word of God. Why the contrast? What happens to the world, the various environments in which God has placed us, when saintliness is the only thing we are after? Obviously the world is placed in the background as something incidental, not quite deserving to be there, like a small child playing with a toy in some remote corner of a conference room. Those in conference do not mind if he is there so long as he does not get in the way. The world is something Protestant piety tolerates so long as its situations and crises do not mar our pilgrimage to saintliness. Such a Christian is therefore in the peculiar position of being placed by God in a world and in a specific environment that he then tries to ignore or put aside. But if God's Word is God's living will addressed to man in every new situation and environment, providing clues and directions for the response to that situation, how dare the Christian ignore those situations for something else such as his own saintliness? The choice is between a pursuit of my goals, my ideals, my virtues, and the appropriate response to and action in the world God has given to me.

Dietrich Bonhoeffer, the German pastor and theologian who was killed by the Nazis in 1945 after two years of imprisonment, records from his prison cell his own rejection of saintliness.

I remember talking to a young French pastor at A. thirteen years ago. We were discussing what our real purpose was in life.

He said he would like to become a saint. I think it is quite likely he did become one. At the time I was very much impressed, though I disagreed with him, and said I should prefer to have faith, or words to that effect. For a long time I did not realize how far we were apart. I thought I could acquire faith by trying to live a holy life, or something like it. . . . Later I discovered and am still discovering up to this very moment that it is only by living completely in this world that one learns to believe. One must abandon every attempt to make something of oneself, whether it be a saint, a converted sinner, a churchman, . . . a righteous man or an unrighteous one, a sick man or a healthy one. This is what I mean by worldliness—taking life in one's stride, with all its duties and problems, its successes and failures, its experiences and helplessness.[34]

Yet in these criticisms of Protestant piety's nose-thumbing treatment of the world, we are really flailing a corpse. Saintliness, Christian virtues, renouncing the world, waiting for the trumpet to sound—all this sounds quaint to contemporary ears. Contemporary Christians do not talk to their children in such terms, nor do they think of their own Christian lives in this way. Protestant piety's mood of world denial is being exchanged for a secular substitute, the pursuit of leisure. The basic contrast in which we live our lives is not earth and heaven, but work and leisure. Similar to the religious piety of world denial and the retreat to the individual concern for the soul and the character is the secular piety of world denial with its retreat from the nonleisure environments. Hence, the contemporary Christian is resentful when the peace and order of the suburban church are interrupted by political controversies, the racial revolution, and problems of labor and management. The church exists in the leisure world and should be a quiet place "near to the heart of God." However happy we are about the displacement of grandmother's otherworldly piety, when we look at its substitute we can only grieve, if not tremble, about what may be next in store.

Chapter Nine

THE ARROGANT TYRANNY
OF UNSELFISHNESS

She's the sort of woman who lives for others—you can always
tell the others by their hunted expression.

—*C. S. Lewis*[35]

A second theme in the docetic or creation-denying mood
of Protestant piety is selflessness or "service." "Others, Lord,
yes others; let this my motto be," was an expression of it in
church hymnody. Similar to the piety of worldlessness, this
piety describes the Christian life by making simple contrasts.
The Christian life is selfless and not selfish. It is for others and
not myself, according to the will of God and not my own will,
giving and not receiving, sacrificing and not being sacrificed
for. The theme of self-denial is probably the dominant theme
in Calvin's description of the Christian life. Whether Calvin
himself meant the term in the creation-denying sense is for
Calvin scholars to debate. The piety that came to dominate
the Protestant churches was incapable of regarding the self
and the will as God's creation. I should clarify that I am using
the word "self" here in both a general and a specific sense.
Generally speaking, the self is the total person. Therefore, a
selfless act is an act that disregards the concerns and needs of
the total person. Specifically, the self is the specific willing,
desiring, yearning, and deciding aspect of the person. Here a
selfless act is an act that attempts to disregard "my desires,"

that which I want, and replaces these desires with the desires
and wants of someone else such as God or neighbor. The frequently used prayer of confession illustrates such selflessness:
"We have followed too much the devices and desires of our
own hearts." Compare this to the phrase from the hymn
"Take My Life, and Let It Be": "Take my *will*, and make it
Thine; It shall be no longer mine."

So, what is wrong with this? The problem is a delicate
one, for such hymns and prayers reflect the Biblically rooted
and indispensable motif of the suffering disciple. Whatever
that motif means, our reaction to its distorted counterpart in
Protestant piety is clear. Protestant piety's view of the "unselfish Christian" is psychologically untenable and theologically
erroneous in that it denies the self as God's good creation and
ignores the way sin permeates "selfless" acts.

The Will Behind the Will

Why is unselfishness psychologically untenable? Let me
recall what was said about "the motives behind the motives"
in Chapter Eight. It appears that in the piety of selflessness,
Protestant piety is doing the same thing it does in its treatment of pure motives. It assumes that the will or the self
works in transparent and easily controllable units. A selfless
act is simply an act for the sake of God or neighbor, and no
more questions need be asked. But to stop questioning is not
only idolatrous but boring. So ask we must. Where does the
subconscious come into the picture? It has long since been
settled that human beings have impulses, drives, and fears of
which they are not conscious and which they will not (or
cannot) admit to themselves. What does such a hidden world
do to the so-called selfless act and the claim that a certain act
is merely for the sake of "others"?

At this point we must recognize a great number of possible
motives for a "selfless" act. Jane Smith's desire to give her-

self to a chaste, single, and sacrificing missionary program in
South India has as part of its background a deep-rooted fear
of men. Sam Jones's insistence on always being the one to pay
for the foursome's dinner has as part of its background a
deep sense of guilt toward one of the parties due to some incident in the distant past. Joe Brown's compulsive insistence
on always being the last one through the door, the one always
to take the cold cup of coffee, and the one always to give in
on which television program to watch has as part of its background the inability of facing his guilt feelings if he acted
any other way. These examples call to mind a line from
Chesterton:

> Most of us have suffered from a certain sort of ladies who, by
> their perverse unselfishness, give more trouble than the selfish;
> who almost clamor for the unpopular dish and scramble for
> the worst seat.[36]

In making this observation of the complexity of the self and
its background, I do not mean to say that the acts in the
above examples are necessarily wrong. It may be quite appropriate for Jane Smith to go to South India, fear of men
or not. The only question raised concerns the pretension of
unselfishness.

"Without His Minding . . ."

I said above that the piety of selflessness denies that the
self is God's creation. Why? Because Protestant piety treats
the desires, the well-being, the "will" of the individual as
something to be ashamed of and to get rid of as soon as possible. "Take my will, and make it Thine; It shall be no longer
mine." Such a prayer makes it sound as though God did not
know what he was doing in creating us the way we are. For
how are we created? We are created organic creatures with
organic desires and wants. (Does the hymn writer want God
to take these over as *his?*) We are created with a will to survive,

and unless we desire to fulfill certain minimum conditions,
such as eating, eliminating, and staying out from under fast-
moving trucks, we shall soon find ourselves very much dead.
We are created with the capacity to set and attain personal
goals, such as competence in some undertaking, certain skills,
or being a certain kind of person. We are also created with
the capacity to enjoy things, and entertain various kinds of
pleasures. C. S. Lewis has put this point as eloquently as anyone when he makes Screwtape complain about God's laxness
with the human race:

> He's a hedonist at heart. . . . There are things for humans to
> do all day long without His minding in the least—sleeping,
> washing, eating, drinking, making love, playing, praying, work-
> ing. . . . He talks of their losing their selves, He means only
> abandoning the clamor of self-will; once they have done that,
> He really gives them back all their personality, and boasts
> . . . that when they are wholly His they will be more themselves
> than ever.[37]

If we are made this way and for these kinds of things, how
dare we talk about our own welfare, our own needs and desires, our own goals and joys as if they were of the devil? The
problem is, of course, complicated by the fact of sin, the corruption of the self and its tendency to worship itself. But even
with that qualification, we cannot escape the fact that the
self is an aspect of God's created world. Therefore, simple
unselfishness, life wholly in service for "others," cannot be a
mark of the Christian life. God does not call us to give up our
wills, our pleasure, or our desires even for him. He made us
able to enjoy and desire, not only himself, but his creation in
which we are placed.

Unselfishness and Demons

Perhaps the most serious problem with the piety of unselfishness concerns the demonic nature of unselfishness. I mean
by this the subtle way in which we human beings can use

unselfishness to promote the self in idolatrous and manipula-
tive ways. This pushes us to the question of the legitimate
and Biblical meaning of self-denial and the suffering disciple.
But first, a distinction:

1. In the psychological sense, all acts are acts *of* the self
and on behalf of the self. Because we are made this way,
"selfishness" in this sense is inevitable and proper.

2. Acting for the *well-being* of the self (its existence and
pleasures) is proper but not an absolute criterion of our acts.
It is always conceivable that the Word of God asks for some
sacrifice of that well-being, perhaps even death. Selfishness in
this situation would be regarding one's own existence, pleasures, and immediate goals as identical with the Word of God
or preferable to the Word of God. This would amount to a
worship of the self, a refusal to take up the cross in suffering
discipleship.

In other words, the self, like any other created entity, can
become an object of worship and a competitor with God. But
the opposite can also happen, so that unselfishness is worshiped and preferred to the Word of God. Two examples may
suffice. "Unselfishness" is frequently a mask for a psychological condition called sado-masochism. This means the deriva-
tion of pleasure (usually some vague sexual pleasure) from
inflicting suffering on another, or from receiving suffering
from another. This enjoyment of suffering can occur at more
subtle levels than conscious and obvious experiences. Hence,
such a person will create situations in which he is insulted or
ignored and will get a strange pleasure out of being always the
one to make the sacrifice. But what is really controlling these
situations of apparent unselfishness is an unacknowledged
self that thrives on torture and suffering and that manipulates
the world and persons to its end.

A second illustration is the tendency of unselfishness to
dominate and control. The act on behalf of another naturally
creates an obligation. When that obligation cannot be met,
the person on the receiving end feels guilty. If such a relation

becomes a set pattern, where Joe always receives from Bill,
Joe soon becomes physically and emotionally dependent on
Bill, virtually under Bill's control. For Joe is never in the
position to question or to fight back. That would be gross
ingratitude to the perpetual "benefactor." The "unselfish"
person, therefore, not only gives and sacrifices, but controls.
If this "unselfishness" is successfully carried out through all
his relationships, he will control them all. The benefactor
approaches the other person as someone merely to help and
therefore control. Hence, the *demonic* nature of unselfishness. For is not this the essence of the demonic, that which
takes over and controls? More in line with true self-denial is
a "selfishness" capable of acknowledging the other person as
a person with his own right to contribute and to help. The
life of grace includes the capacity to place ourselves in the
hands of our brothers, to be dependent on them and receive
from them. The demand always to be the benefactor is a refusal to recognize our brothers and ourselves as mutually related. Therefore, it turns out to be a demand to be God to our
brothers, the worst demonry of all.

It seems hardly necessary to observe that the piety of unselfishness is fast being displaced. Hymns that beseech God
to "take my will" sound as quaint to the modern ear as the
other hymns of Protestant piety. For what is the piety of unselfishness being exchanged? What is taking the place of
service, life for others, and giving the will to God? The picture is not very clear. I can only venture a guess. Most contemporary Christians appear to feel that life should include
efforts on behalf of causes other than their own individual or
family problems. This vague uneasiness drives many into
church activities: into church school teaching, men's groups,
Boy Scout leadership, and the circles. Such seems to be the
present-day version of "commitment of one's will to God."
If so, can we be satisfied with such a substitute? Is this really
the legitimate and Biblical self-denial, the piety of the suffering disciple?

PART II

*The Displacement of
Protestant Piety*

Chapter Ten

PILGRIM'S PROGRESS

PIETY: "What moved you at first to betake yourself to a pilgrim's life?"
CHRISTIAN: "I was driven out of my native country by a dreadful sound that was in mine ears; to wit, that unavoidable destruction did attend me, if I abode in that place where I was."

—*John Bunyan*[38]

In Chapters One through Eight, I have set forth some of the marks of Protestant piety. There are more, of course. We have, however, considered enough of them to illustrate the main thesis that Protestant piety is quickly disappearing. Now for a new question: What gives Protestant piety its unity? If we could answer this, the thesis concerning the collapse of Protestant piety would be clearer. The problem before us in the present chapter is the unity, the total landscape, of Protestant piety. I shall try to paint a picture of this landscape in three steps which are the three elements in any pilgrimage.

Goals, Progress, and Disciplines

The most fundamental fact about Protestant piety is that it is just like Catholic piety in its general structure. In com-

mon to both Catholic and Protestant piety or versions of the
Christian life is the notion that the Christian life is a pilgrimage. That is, making a pilgrimage from one place to another
provides us with a fairly accurate metaphor for describing
the sort of thing the Christian life is. We find the pilgrimage
theme in the favorite hymns of Protestant piety: "O use me,
Lord, use even me, Just as Thou wilt, and when, and where;
Until Thy blessed face I see, Thy rest, Thy joy, Thy glory
share."[39] We testify to the pilgrimage of the Christian life
when we sing, "Lead on, O king Eternal," "Jesus, Saviour,
pilot me," "Jesus, lead the way," "He leadeth me" "Far off
I see the goal," and many others. Insofar as the Protestant way
is a pilgrimage, John Bunyan's *The Pilgrim's Progress* might
be *the* classic symbol and expression of Protestant piety.

Furthermore, three specific elements are necessary for the
Christian life to be a pilgrimage. The first is a *definite goal of
the pilgrimage*. The *ultimate* goal in both Catholic and Protestant piety is the vision of God, or, as Protestant theologians
described it, glorification. Such is the theme of most of the
hymns cited above. However, both pieties agree that the
Christian life also reaches toward a goal realizable in the
present life. The Catholic traditions call it saintliness. Protestant piety used to call it "a righteous, godly, and sober life."
The first condition of the pilgrimage view of the Christian
life is a fairly clear and detailed conception of this goal or
end, attainable at least partially in the present life. In short,
Protestant piety includes a detailed picture of what every
Christian is aiming at. The previous nine chapters comprise
an attempt to set forth this picture. Therefore, the goal of the
Christian life is a life according to certain Christian principles, grounded in unselfish motives, resulting in specific religious acts, behaviors, duties, and virtues.

The second element in the pilgrimage metaphor is the
pilgrimage itself. The Christian life is a journey toward, a
progress toward, a definite goal. In short, the Christian life

is the progress of a pilgrim. In the Victorian phase of Protestant piety, roughly the last half of the nineteenth and the
beginning of the twentieth centuries, the religious education
movement took place in American Protestantism. This movement provided Protestant piety with a specific way of conceiving the pilgrimage, namely, that of "growth" or "nurture." The piety of nurture differed from earlier Protestant
orthodox and Puritan views by placing the emphasis on the
conditions of growth and on the nurturing influences, such
as the family. Puritan ethics saw the pilgrimage of the Christian faith much more as occurring by means of individual
disciplines such as prayer and Bible study. The important
point, however, is that the Christian's attitude toward his
own life is an expectation of improvement and spiritual ad-
vancement. He can expect that prayer, Bible study, Christian
education, and Sunday worship will have a cumulative effect.
He should be closer to the goal after twenty years than after
ten. The Catholic version of this is that certain "habits" are
built up and supernatural virtues infused.

The third element in the pilgrimage metaphor is that there
are specific *things to do* to attain the goal. Therefore, an important part of Catholic and Protestant piety covers the
specific religious disciplines by which the Christian travels
toward the goal. Two classics out of the literature of Anglican
and Puritan piety should help illustrate the point. Jeremy
Taylor, the seventeenth-century English bishop, wrote in
1650 and 1651 *Holy Living* and *Holy Dying,* thus covering
"the complete duty of a Christian." A large part of *Holy
Living* is devoted to "instruments and means of the holy life."
These "means" include reading and studying the Scriptures,
fasting, keeping the festivals, prayer and devotions, the care of
one's time, and practicing the presence. The writer has much
to say about the times and types of prayer, detailed techniques
of worship, etc. Richard Baxter, a Puritan contemporary of
Jeremy Taylor, wrote his *Christian Directory* also in the

seventeenth century, one fourth of which was devoted to "private duties." Baxter's great concern is to show his reader "how." He not only exhorts Christians to trust in God but he gives "fifteen directions for a quieting and comforting Trust in God." He not only exhorts belief in the Holy Ghost and subjecting one's soul to God; he writes chapters on "How to believe in the Holy Ghost and live by his Grace," and "How to bring the soul in subjection of God."[40] Reminiscent of such detailed exercises are the exhortations still heard occasionally from the pulpit to give one's "time, talent, and possessions."

In summary, the Christian life is thought of in Protestant piety as something demanding specific day-by-day disciplines, if not even skills. These exercises are employed as means of traveling toward the goal of Christian holiness. This pilgrimage piety is common both to Catholicism and Protestantism. Catholicism gives far more weight to the Sacraments as "means," especially the Eucharist, and also to contemplation. Protestantism places more stress on the Bible, its study and proclamation, and on self-examination.

The Inflexible Perfectionism of the Pilgrim Way

Are there any marks or characteristics of the pilgrimage itself? In Protestantism's version of the Christian life three general marks are especially prominent. We have already observed these in preceding chapters. Now we shall put them together. *Individualism* is the first mark of the Protestant pilgrimage. The pilgrimage of the Christian life is a pilgrimage of the individual to *his* goal. The question about the Christian life is always cast in this manner. What ought *I* to be? What ought *I* to do? When the question is so stated, everything else in the Christian life exists for the sake of *my* piety. I must love others because I ought to be that sort of person. I should vote for fair-housing practices because that act will further secure *my* Christian character. Whatever we say in criticism of individualism, the point is not that all "I" questions are wrong. Rather, there are other questions that can be asked and other ways of thinking about the Christian life.

The second general mark of pilgrimage piety is its *perfectionism.* I do not mean by perfectionism that such piety has within it an express doctrine of Christian perfection in the present life. But it does contain perfectionist overtones. The whole means-to-ends approach says in effect: To attain B, do A; to be a Christian, do the following; to live a devout and holy life, engage in these disciplines. This approach obviously leaves out a great deal. How do I know that these goals which I regard as *the* goals of the Christian life are the only ones, or the right ones? Is it not possible that I, in my sin, misconceive the goals? Is it not possible that the ever-changing circumstances of life force me to suspend certain goals? If so, is the Christian life describable simply as a fulfilling of personal ends through personal disciplines?[41]

A third general mark of the Protestant version of pilgrimage piety is *inflexibility.* If the Christian life means an advance toward a clearly known goal (holiness, etc.) through specific means, how can it ever be life in response to the living Word of God? The implication is that God's living Word is simply synonymous with those goals fixed in and by the past. If that is the case, the Word is not the living presence of Jesus Christ in his Spirit. The Word is a fixed goal and as such is not living, but dead. Protestant piety turns out to be life in a fixed circle of duties and virtues. Incapable of breaking out of that circle, the Protestant Christian is unable to come to grips with new and complex situations in his life: the constant change of cultural patterns, the bursting forth of hitherto unimaginable possibilities and crises. Caught in inflexible patterns of taboos and duties, the Victorian pietist faces the rest of Christendom and the changing world with a rather pathetic helplessness. He cannot make room in his pilgrimage for African Christians who dress in quasi-nudity, for Anglican Christians who celebrate the Lord's Supper with real wine, or for the Japanese Christians who are outside the institutional church. Nor can he make room for unashamed activity in and through the great agencies of power, or for the weird world of the modern teen-ager with his myriads of new problems. In short, Protestant piety had very little self-criticism built into it. Its pilgrimage structure forced it always to face the same direction and plod toward the same goal.

Chapter Eleven

THE DECLINE AND FALL
OF PROTESTANT PIETY

The sea of faith
Was once, too, at the full, and round earth's shore
Lay like the folds of a bright girdle furl'd;
But now I only hear
Its melancholy, long, withdrawing roar,
Retreating . . .

—Matthew Arnold

Who fluctuate idly without term or scope,
Of whom each strives, nor knows for what he strives,
And each half lives a hundred different lives.

—Matthew Arnold[42]

And now it is gone—or at least quickly going. Protestant piety was carried away by the same winds that swept away Christian Endeavor, the great pulpit orators such as Henry Ward Beecher, and the powerful congregations of the central city with their magnificent church edifices.

Symptoms of the Decline of Protestant Piety

How do we know Protestant piety is gone or going? By what evidence dare we lay this ghost? By looking fearlessly into our own souls, and by looking around us at the churches and at the culture.

No Longer Pilgrims. The depth and radicality of the change is revealed when we remember the pilgrimage nature of Protestant piety. The Christian life as a pilgrimage toward devoutness through the means of personal disciplines is the heart and soul of Protestant piety. It provided the canvas on which the Christian life was painted, or, to change metaphors, the framework of the building of Christian life. Now, those vestiges of Protestant piety which are still around function outside the framework of the pilgrimage. A good example is prayer. Within Protestant piety, prayer was a regular activity of the Christian life, for it was an indispensable means to the goal. In prayer, Christians battled with the devil, engaged in day-by-day, minute-by-minute struggles with temptation, gained new strength and consolation, all toward the *goal* of holiness, personal purity, and Christian character. Prayer, in brief, was a regular exercise with a definite purpose. The twentieth-century Christian still prays, but prayer for him is not a necessary or regular part of a lifelong pilgrim's progress. It is an occasional phenomenon, existing in the formalities of institutional worship or in the terrors of a crisis situation. It has a purpose, of course, but the purpose is an immediate one—not a long-range one, as in pilgrimage piety. Prayer is more the occasional outcry. It is not, as in Protestant piety, a discipline or exercise or "means."

In a nutshell it appears that the twentieth-century Christian simply has no clear goal toward which the Christian life leads, the pursuing of which gives point to his religious activities. He has life goals, of course: a successful career, health, children, a secure retirement. Without any special religious goal toward which he hopes to progress, regular day-by-day religious exercises have little point. Hence, what religious acts the twentieth-century Christian does perform tend to be ends in themselves or else have some extrareligious purpose.

Me-Tooism. We have already considered the bulk of the evidence for the collapse of Protestant piety in our analysis of the various marks of Protestant piety. In most cases we tried to show that some traditional aspect of Protestant piety was no longer very meaningful to contemporary Christians and that it therefore had been exchanged for something else. Hence, religious experience is traded for aesthetic feelings; religious duties and acts, for religious activities about the church; Christian principles, for general national and cultural principles; etc. In short, the exchange has substituted for the marks of traditional Protestant piety a piety that is either secular but retaining the vocabulary and trappings of religion, or just frankly secular. In Chapter Thirteen, I should like to take up the secular substitutes in some detail.

Perhaps the clearest evidence for the fact of this exchange is that twentieth-century Christians turn everywhere else but to a religious resource for *every* kind of serious problem. Historians have been saying for ages how science has displaced religion as a way of explaining certain things. With the coming of the social sciences a new step is taken. Science now displaces religion as the way the fundamental *human* problems are met. I do not want to give the impression here that the Christian gospel exists merely to "solve human problems." Christians will always insist that the glorification of God is the real point of the Christian gospel, and no human science can replace that.

However, the gospel does claim to affect us at the level of specific sins, acts, and attitudes. Does not Paul exhort, "Let all bitterness and wrath and anger and clamor and slander be put away from you" (Eph. 4:31)? Is not the gospel addressed to such matters as the sting of death, freedom, the capacity to love God and one's neighbor, life within marriage and the family, and, above all, to the fundamental problem of sin which requires man to undergo a new birth? The depth and completeness of the exchange of Protestant piety for something else comes home to us when we remember that the automatic reflex of the contemporary Christian in trouble is to get help from some medical or social science. Divorce, despair, suicide, psychological misery, worry about death, a scandalous immorality—all prompt us into the offices of the marriage counselors and psychiatrists. Even when we seek the office of the religious professional, the minister, we do so hoping he has psychiatric and social work tools at his finger-tips.

In its day, Protestant piety played its role, perhaps the central role, as a resource for dealing with the deepest problems of the human being: *consolation* when life falls in; *reconciliation* between individuals (such as man and wife, parents and children, quarreling friends); *reconstruction* of the weakened and distorted, such as emotional collapse, guilt, paralyzing fear; and *re-creation* of new and living perspectives and attitudes on things. If nothing else is clear in these chapters, this much should be. The real source and resource of these things, *for Protestant Christians themselves,* is no longer Protestant piety. The resourcefulness of man himself proves to be more efficient and more successful in these matters than the Christian life in the form of Protestant piety. The work of consolation, reconciliation, reconstruction, and re-creation is undertaken enthusiastically by marriage counselors, psychiatrists, artists, social workers, public school teachers, government agencies, the Peace Corps, the Job Corps, the war on poverty, in short, society tapping its own resources for the reconstitution of the human being.

This leaves the Protestant churches caught in an almost impossible dilemma. They can justify their existence by appealing to their otherworldly function, giving up any stake in man's earthly career, concerned only with "pie in the sky by and by." Or they can attempt to compete with society's endeavors, a competition that turns out to be a reproduction and imitation of those endeavors at a small and inefficient level. Or to put the dilemma another way, the church can either become the cultic fringe of the activities of culture, or it can try to become one more agency for human welfare running after society's endeavors crying, "Me too." If the former way is taken, the church and its message tend to be superfluous to the concrete problems of the human being (the griefs and disruptions and helplessness that call for consolation and reconciliation and reconstruction). If the latter way is taken, the church and its message become simply superfluous. That is, since society shows itself more able to deal with these problems through its own agencies of power and wealth, it does not need to duplicate itself in another vast institution such as the church.

However much we dwell on the "otherworldliness" of traditional Protestant piety, we must admit that in its time it did have crucial effects on human society and on human beings. It really did function to console and reconcile and reconstruct. Now it functions primarily as a verbal tradition, providing a way of *talking* about religion and mankind and values. What it does not do is to serve as the concretization of faith, a powerful resource for actual problems, an interpretive guide for decisions that count. In other words it is no longer a living *piety*.

This breakdown of Protestant piety (a concrete and detailed pattern in which faith can express itself) helps explain a great deal about the contemporary church. This is why the hymns make little sense to us and our singing of them is "vain repetition." This is why no clear pattern of "religious training" of children is available. It explains the many in college and seminary whose impulses and intentions are "Christian," but who are deeply stung by a skepticism that leaves them wondering what Christian doctrine and the Christian life are all about.

Explanations for the Decline of Protestant Piety

I ask now what may be a fruitless question: Why this breakdown of Protestant piety? Granting the evidence for it, how do we explain it? One explanation we dare not exclude, and

yet we hesitate to include it. Could it be that the decline of
Protestant piety is God's judgment on Protestant piety? Built
into every idolatry are sources of its destruction. If this is the
case, we need not think that because Protestant piety is going,
the Christian faith is doomed. The destruction of Protestant
piety may be the necessary prelude to a new and vigorous expression of the faith. Yet, speaking about the judgment of
God still leaves much unsaid in the way of explanation, for
God judges through historical forces. We must still ask, What
specifically has brought about the decline of Protestant piety?

Theological Shouts and Theological Silences. It is always
very difficult to assess the effect of intellectual currents on
history. More specifically, it is difficult to assess the way theology affects (and is affected by) the life of the church. Some
affecting is obvious. Therefore, Reformation theology played
a significant role in the formation of Protestant piety. For instance, the piety of the Sacred Page is not unrelated to theological battles between Reformers and Roman Catholics
concerning the authority of the Bible and its place in the
church.

We should not therefore be surprised that theology plays
some role in the decline of Protestant piety. Telling blows
against this piety have been struck from the theological camp.
The social gospel movement, beginning in the Victorian era
itself, raised serious questions about the "individualism" of
Protestant piety. The rise of historical ways of dealing with
the Bible made impossible the appeal to the Bible as an
authoritarian code of law. Theology's listening to and re-
flecting the moods of other disciplines such as philosophy,
sociology, and Freudian psychology helped annihilate the
"unimpeachable conduct" of the Victorian gentleman. Perhaps most important of all were the "new reformation" theologies of a generation ago, which, like Luther, grounded all
thought about the Christian life in the justification by grace
through faith. The resulting emphasis was on man's sinful-

ness, helplessness, and need for God's forgiving act. More recently has been the rise of a theological ethics that sees the Christian life, not so much in terms of principles, sanctions, norms, and laws, but the more elusive terms of response, context, and freedom.

Yet theology must take responsibility for more than just the criticisms of Protestant piety. It also shares the responsibility for the present vacuum of true piety and the transition of Protestant piety into merely secular substitutes. Our present situation is due in part to theological failure, the lack of positive theological thought and leadership in the area of the Christian life. The total import of theology in this area is largely negative. Under the pounding of theological criticism, we learned we could not easily identify this act and that principle with the living Word of God. The mind-set this produced was a skepticism about the knowledge of God and God's will in concrete situations. To put it another way, the new theologies of the Word passed over a theology of the Spirit of God whereby God's presence in concrete situations could be apprehended. There is simply no way at all to testify to God's concrete, actual will or Word that would not sound idolatrous. No feeling, principle, intellectual reflection, or pattern could be identified with God's actual Word. The alternative is that we simply live without his Word. These theologies bludgeoned down upon the simple pieties of Victorian Christianity, but little time was required for them to produce a cliché world of their own. How long can one stand to hear about God "acting in events," his Word "breaking in," personal encounter, the historical nature of Christianity, and the context of decision?

Under theological criticism, we learned that we could not simply regard a text of Scripture as a law, a simple directive for action. Yet contemporary theology has not given any clear suggestion as to how Scripture can be used as a source or guide for the Christian life. Contemporary theologians agree that

Scripture is an "authority," and that the living Word speaks in it and through it. Yet the road is a long one from that sort of observation to a constructive doctrine of the role of Scripture in the Christian life. The same could be said about Protestant criticisms of natural law. Constructive suggestions are still lacking as to what consideration we are to give to the body, the self, the world, and the "nature of man," in the Christian life.

The Cultural Displacement. The second kind of explanation of the decline of Protestant piety is sociological. We have already talked at some length about cultural changes. The most significant cultural happening in the decline of Protestant piety is the rise of the social sciences and other institutions devoted to human betterment. Philosophies such as existentialism offer a "philosophical faith" and a way for a human being to reflect on his deepest problems. Doctors and psychiatrists not only address themselves to the body's illnesses but also to deeply rooted psychological problems demanding a totally new orientation or "new birth." (Does it sound familiar?) Economists, political scientists, congressmen, city planners, and labor consultants work on problems produced by group conflicts all the way from war to fair employment practices. Furthermore, while they may not always solve these problems, they work at their resolution more skillfully and efficiently than their religious competitors. In other words, many of the problems for which Protestant piety offered solutions and reconciliations are dealt with more successfully by more powerful, more wealthy, and more scientifically oriented institutions.

A more specific sociological clue is found in what is happening to the church. In traditional Protestant piety, the congregation was the place in which or from which the Christian life was lived. Bible study, worship, and various religious exercises all occurred within a small and unchanging congregation that was made up of lifelong companions. Marriage in such a congregation was a real event, and so was baptism, and so was burial. All this provided a personal setting and a stable background in which piety could "progress." In place of this small, stable congregation has come a very large, largely impersonal institution. Many in that institution move into and out of the congregation every year. The attempts of the institution to overcome the impersonal relationships produced by its size and instability turn out to be artificial and sporadic attempts at togetherness. The people in the small Puritan congregation were "together" because they believed much the same things, practiced much the same things, and knew each other over a long period of years. The people in the large suburban church are not united either by orthodox doctrines or by being pilgrims in an agreed-on framework of piety. They are together in "activities." The church congregation, in other words, is no longer the place where piety is pursued and strengthened. In saying this I am not idealizing the traditional congregation or scorning everything about contemporary patterns. I am only trying to understand why what has happened has happened.

Chapter Twelve

SEVEN OTHER SPIRITS

When the unclean spirit has gone out of a man, he passes through waterless places seeking rest, but he finds none. Then he says, "I will return to my house from which I came." And when he comes he finds it empty, swept, and put in order. Then he goes and brings with him seven other spirits more evil than himself, and they enter and dwell there; and the last state of that man becomes worse than the first. So shall it be also with this evil generation.

—*Matthew 12:43–45*

If Protestant piety is dying, what is replacing it? In each chapter, I observed remnants of the old piety, present, however, in new ways. Yet such talk is really misleading. Recall the point made in Chapter One that faith unavoidably must express itself in concrete attitudes and acts. Furthermore, these attitudes and acts need some organizing pattern that is rooted in the gospel—in short, a piety. If Protestant piety is exchanged for another *piety*, this must mean another pattern organizing the total life of the Christian. The vestiges or remainders of Protestant piety (aesthetic emotions, church activities, and the rest) are not themselves total patterns like the Protestant pilgrimage to the devout life. Has some unifying pattern now replaced Protestant piety, functioning for twentieth-century American Christians much as Protestant piety served our Puritan and Victorian ancestors? If we mean

by piety an organizing pattern of the Christian life which is
the genuine expression of Biblical faith, the answer seems
to be negative. No piety analogous to traditional Protestant
piety now exists for American Christendom as a whole. Perhaps some individuals and groups live by such a piety. That
is not the typical situation. Hence, we face a very serious
problem. Faith inevitably must express itself in *some* concrete
way. The value of traditional Protestant and Catholic piety
was that each offered specific directives, derived in part at
least from the Biblical witness, which guided and unified
faith's expressions. The present situation is serious because
no genuine piety exists that might serve as such a guide or
directive. Faith is called to express itself in a vacuum without
the organizing pattern of a genuine piety.

Piety, Genuine and Pseudo

Note the distinction between a genuine and a pseudo piety.
Genuine piety always has the three following characteristics:
(1) It is an organizing pattern of faith's obedience, whose
unity is given to it by some aspect of the gospel. (2) As an
"organizing pattern," genuine piety includes and organizes
the total life of the Christian, not merely some aspect of the
human being such as the intellect, the activities, or the emotions, and not merely some phase of human culture. The
obedience effected by faith, while it is never absolutely pure,
tends always toward inclusiveness, influencing the human
being as such, in his relationships, his leisure, values, voca-
tion, etc. (3) Genuine piety really is an expression of *faith*.
This means that the fundamental impulse toward expression
is an interior and spontaneous one, rather than simply the
product of some institutional or cultural planning. Genuine
piety, in other words, occurs at the conjunction of true faith
impelled to expression, an actual cultural and historical situation, and the contemporary witness of the Spirit of God. This
implies that genuine piety cannot be artificially produced.

It cannot be whipped up by theologians or passed down from central headquarters through the institutional hierarchy of the church. Genuine piety always has, of course, a historical and cultural expression. However, unless these expressions make some connection with faith itself so that they really serve to express faith, we are not talking about genuine piety, but about something else.

Because of this threefold nature of genuine piety, pseudo piety is of several kinds, depending on which characteristic is lacking. It is pseudo if it retains the external trappings and vocabulary of religion without the actual content of the gospel. An example might be the happiness of the peace of mind cult whose actual content has little to do with the good news of Jesus Christ. Secondly, a piety might be pseudo if it affected or organized only some phase or aspect of human life, for instance the intellect, or social relationships, or simply the emotions. Thirdly, a piety might be pseudo if it does express in its content something of the gospel, and does reflect an organizing pattern of life in its totality, yet remains simply a pattern imposed upon the Christian from without, making no contact at all with interior faith and its powerful striving for expression. An example might be an ecclesiastical gimmick programmed by the powers that be, for the purpose of tapping and organizing the energies of Christian people; for instance, some program according to which Christians are assigned a pattern of church activity in small study groups. Such a pattern might look like a piety insofar as it claims to describe what it means to be a Christian in the twentieth century. However, instead of being an expression of interior faith, it is merely an organization of exterior activities.

Let me try to summarize the thesis of the present chapter in three brief statements:

1. Traditional Protestant piety has ceased to be the organizing pattern of the Christian life; hence we are now living in a vacuum of genuine piety.

2. Faith inevitably lives outward, expressing itself in the concrete attitudes, acts, and decisions of the faithful person. Without a meaningful and genuine piety available, Christians are drawn to various pseudo pieties that are available.

3. Two kinds of pseudo pieties dominate the Protestant-American scene. The first are *secular* pseudo pieties such as the cult of happiness or superpatriotism. The second are *religious* pseudo pieties such as church renewal or "Christian existentialism."

In the present chapter, I shall attempt to describe certain *secular* pseudo pieties which, like the seven spirits of the parable, are sweeping in to fill the empty house left by Protestant piety. Almost all the secular pseudopieties on the American scene are in some way or other expressions of one basic phenomenon. Some writers describe it as a fourth religion (besides Protestantism, Catholicism, and Judaism), namely, "American religion."[43] This fourth religion is a "culture religion" because the values and characteristics of American culture provide this religion with its basic content. The theologians and sociologists who write about the new religion have different ways of classifying its types. Martin Marty divides it into cultural religion, political religion, social religion, and psychological religion. Roy Eckardt finds within this general cultural religion a folk religion, a cult of reassurance, a suburban piety, a piety of patriotism and free enterprise, and revivalism. I would like to illustrate the exchange of Protestant piety for secular piety by selecting two of these secular pseudo pieties: the happiness piety of the cult of reassurance, and the piety of superpatriotism.

The Innocuous Piety of the Happiness Cult

Since William Miller's devastating article "Some Negative Thinking About Norman Vincent Peale," additional criticisms of Dr. Peale are superfluous. And this is not my intention here. But as we learned in the Krebiozen case, refuting something scientifically and convincing its adherents are two very different matters. Pealism may be exposed as chaff. It is still very difficult to blow away. In the case of the happiness cult, Dr. Peale is not so much the perpetrator of the crime as its chief symbol and formulator. Even without him, this pseudo piety would be a powerful competitor for the impulses of faith. In the long run it may be the most powerful competitor of all. Among the various pseudo pieties available, the happiness cult alone resembles Protestant piety in its pilgrimage structure. Like Protestant piety, happiness piety has individualistic and clearly definable goals (confidence, lack of worry, a cheerful mood, etc.), as well as specific exercises by which the goals are secured. Are we confused about what it means specifically to be a Christian and to live the Christian life? Do we want to know what to do about it now, this very moment? Happiness piety has answers to these questions. Like the diet ads, it can cite thousands of instances where the program was tried successfully. No wonder happiness piety is so appealing. Unlike ministers, theologians, and Sunday school teachers, it really *can* tell us what to do and be. And who doesn't want to be happy? For many, therefore, the secular ideal of mental and emotional security with its self-help gimmicks provides the substitute for the living of a "godly, righteous, and sober life."

The Dangerous Piety of Superpatriotism

Perhaps the most powerful religion throughout the world today is what Eckhardt calls *folk religion* and what Marty terms political religion. The causes and forces that most excite the populations of the world seem to be those which concern the destiny of their nations. The phenomenon is not limited to young African, Asian, or South American nations. Many Americans approach the American heritage almost in a spirit of worship. Furthermore, we do not see the international conflict merely as an East-West conflict. Rather, we see it as occurring between America and God on the one hand and Russia and evil on the other. And this is what a *folk* religion is. Whenever a people simply take it for granted that "god," the object of their worship, is always on their side and never against them, we have *folk* religion. This kind of "god" is simply a mirror of the *Volk,* the spirit of the people. He functions solely to protect that people and its values. To oppose that people is to oppose its god. To oppose the god is to oppose the people. A good example of a *folk* religion in the Old Testament is the Canaanite religion of Baalism. An equally good example of a nonfolk religion is Hebrew religion. God could be and often was in opposition to the Hebrews. He was not merely a sounding board for their concerns, values, or national characteristics. "Hear the word of the Lord, O people of Israel; for the Lord has a controversy with the inhabitants of the land." (Hos. 4:1.)

Now, we should not be surprised to find in any nation certain people who, lacking any other object of worship, simply worship the nation and its heritage. The welfare and power of the nation is for them the absolute good. So thought European Fascists in World War II. But Fascism is not a mere political philosophy, something comparable to being a Republican or a Democrat. Rather, the fascist mentality latches on to an economic or social tradition in the past that is believed to be the essence of national existence and says, in effect, that the nation, even in the sense of the majority of the people, has no right to deviate from the tradition. All those who hold views different from its own are accused of subversion, of unpatriotic behavior, of being enemies who deserve persecution.

The difference between such Fascism and democracy is a difference in both theory and practice. A fascist state is beyond criticism in theory, because the state is the absolute good, and

thus it cannot tolerate criticism in practice. Those who speak
critically of the revered tradition or who would follow a tradition different from it are branded as enemies and traitors.
As in the piety of the Sacred Page, in which the Bible is
venerated, so the nation becomes an object of worship and,
hence, replaces God.

In contrast, true democracy sees the nation as a delicate
balance of many competing voices, all of which have a right
to exist, and none of which can be permitted to force submis-
sion on others. Decisions are made by the constant adjustment
of these voices and powers to one another, and harmony is
achieved because each respects the others' right to be. A democracy is never perfect, but it never pretends to perfection
as an absolutist state does. So the theory of a democratic state
offers a safeguard against the idolatry that is the essence of a
totalitarian state.

A democracy has the advantage of having built into it processes by which it can change direction, be self-corrective, and
meet new crises. In democratic theory, those who disagree
with one another as to which direction should be taken are
not necessarily enemies plotting against one another or against
the nation. Such disagreement and struggle between repre-
sentative groups (over different economic theories, different
ways of balancing central and local power, different foreign
policies) are the very essence of democracy, in both theory
and practice.

Against this tradition, however, the present-day superpatriots seek to impose a unity of political and social belief
on all Americans, a unity they claim is derived from the
"true Americanism" of our founding fathers. This develop-
ment is not only tragic, but somewhat ironical, since our
founding fathers engaged in vigorous debate and artful compromise in the forming of our Constitution. And though this
"Americanism" faith is by no means new, it is nevertheless
almost humorous that an attempt should be made to isolate
"true Americanism" out of the melting pot and welter of

tongues, cultures, and political and social viewpoints that
have been accepted and absorbed in the course of our national history. *The new Ku Klux*
In the view of the superpatriots, the great majority of
Americans (including the United States Government itself)
are "un-American." Sometimes when the superpatriot groups
come into control of a community, freedom of speech is virtually eliminated, people lose their jobs, the school system is
harassed, curricula censored, libraries revised, and ministers
pressured to leave their churches. And there frequently are
heard frenzied accusations pertaining to plots to overthrow
the Government. For what reason? Because there is actual
evidence of plotting to overthrow the Government by force
and violence? No. For ideological disagreement with the superpatriots! The irony in all this is that if superpatriotism
had its way, a pattern of life would be introduced in America
almost exactly like the pattern in Russia, which the superpatriots themselves hold as the antithesis of America. Thus,
the superpatriots are in the peculiar position of producing
the very state of affairs they say they oppose.

Superpatriotism, as a quasi religion, is not a rare phenomenon in history or among the nations of the world. The
deification of the Egyptian Pharaoh and the Roman emperor,
the Japanese cult of Shinto, and the "German Christians"
who (perhaps for quite different reasons) gave a religious
apologetic for the Nazi regime are all examples of it. Superpatriotism and religion have merged before in America with
great resultant mischief, and there are disturbing signs that
such an amalgamation is under way once again. Some strands
of superpatriotism and Protestant Christianity of a radically
conservative stripe have now united in what is virtually one
movement. Listen to the names of some of the organizations:
The Christian Crusade (Oklahoma), the Twentieth Century
Reformation Hour (New Jersey), the Church League of
America (Illinois), and the Circuit Riders (Ohio).

How widespread is the appeal of these groups? If the argu-

ment of these studies is correct, it may become very widespread and surely will not stay on the fringes of fanaticism,
as we often complacently suppose. If we are living in a
vacuum of genuine piety, Christians will be easily attracted
to movements that talk in the clichés of patriotism and traditional religion, that offer concrete schemes of action, and
that seem to be on the "right" side (America and God). The
superpatriot movement is particularly dangerous at this
point. Let us try to see why:

1. The superpatriot groups have built up through the
years a sizable literature of books, pamphlets, articles in journals such as the *Christian Beacon,* and testimony that gets
into *The Congressional Record.* Much of this literature assumes the discredited method of guilt by association, con-
demning as Communists people who were members of Com-
munist-infiltrated organizations at a time when most Americans were quite ignorant of such infiltration. Much of the
literature provides "proof," not for Communist viewpoints,
but for "collectivist" viewpoints, under which would fall
most of the present Republican and Democratic members of
Congress and, in fact, everyone outside superpatriotism.
Much that has been disproved is still cited simply because the
case was at one time the object of congressional investigation.
Much is just superstition (such as the talk about the Revised
Standard Version of the Bible being a Communist Bible).
However, this literature of erroneous accusation bulks large
in quantity, and the superpatriots continue to publish "docu-
mented" works with many quotations and impressively long
bibliographies. The quotes and documentation frequently
turn out to be from pamphlets and books previously published by the superpatriots. Their claims are "proved" by
simply quoting themselves.[44]

2. The second seductive method employed by the superpatriots is a fallacious either-or logic. The impression the
reader (or hearer of their radio broadcasts) gets is that he is

either a patriotic, Bible-believing, Communist-hating Christian who agrees entirely with the superpatriots, *or* he is "soft on Communism" and an un-American, atheistic collectivist. Could there be a more dangerous rhetorical device than this? Especially does it tempt those who do not have the energy, the time, or the means to investigate further, and who are already searching for a pattern of attitudes and acts to make faith concrete.

3. Equally seductive is the vocabulary of Protestant piety and revivalism in which the superpatriots make their case. The reader is exhorted to pray for the cause. God (the Bible) is constantly quoted, and appeals concerning the "Bible message of personal and individual salvation" are set in the midst of seemingly political pamphlets or books. All this gives the impression that the only concern the superpatriots have is the will of God. Hence their idolatrous identification of God and their own interpretation of the American way of life, their wholesale condemnation (and when possible suppression) or viewpoints not their own, their methods of half-truth, slander; and the Gestapo-like keeping of lists, collecting of weapons, and making unofficial investigations of the more extremist groups—all this gets covered over by the smoke screen of pious clichés.

Let us be clear. There is such a thing as genuine patriotism —of this let there be no doubt. Superpatriotism, however, is a separate phenomenon, existing above ordinary political decisions. Therefore, the issue here is not an issue between our two major political parties. It is not an issue between conservatives and liberals. Nor is it the issue about the powers of the central government, or whether or not we are to resist Communism. Superpatriotism is a phenomenon that must be disassociated from these real political issues and seen for what it is; a nationalistic religion that derives its power from hating and fearing something, and that competes with other pseudo pieties in the present vacuum of genuine piety.

Chapter Thirteen

THE RELIGIOUS PIETIES
OF OFFICIAL CHRISTENDOM

Why, you fool, it's the educated readers who *can* be gulled. All our difficulty comes with the others. When did you meet a workman who believes the papers? He takes it for granted that they're all propaganda and skips the leading articles.

—*C. S. Lewis*[45]

I'd had enough talk and people for a week. Talk is not my line. . . . When you're talking a lot you haven't time to get the words right. Talk is lies.

—*Joyce Cary*[46]

The decline of piety is not a phenomenon limited to the church at large or to the so-called laity. Ours is not a situation of secular pieties in the pew and genuine piety in the pulpit, the seminary, or denominational headquarters. The decline of Puritan and Victorian piety cuts across all Christendom including "official" Christendom. Yet there do seem to be some differences between "lay" and "official" Christendom in the matter of piety. Official Christendom (those who are professionally trained for the church, who preach, publish journals, write books, run conferences, and teach in schools) is in a certain way aware of what has happened. Especially is it aware of the power and extent of the secular pieties. With certain exceptions the reaction of official Christendom to the secular pseudo pieties is negative. Norman Vincent Peale, folk religion, and the vague feeling that "religion" and "faith" are important are often the targets of attack in church publications and religious books.

But where does this leave official Christendom itself? Sensing the absence of Protestant piety and its replacement by dangerous secular pieties, official Christendom attempts to produce a piety of its own in competition with the secular pieties. In other words, pieties have arisen within official Christendom that are neither traditional Protestant piety nor secular piety. I am calling them "religious" pieties in that they *appear* to express genuine themes of the gospel. In the long run, this may not be the case. For the purpose of illustration, I shall attempt to describe three of these pieties which reside in official Christendom and which official Christendom is attempting to transfer to the church at large. For want of better names, I am calling them *empty prophetism, Christian existentialism,* and *renewal activism.*

The Negative Piety of Theological Prophets

Paul Tillich has distinguished between the "Protestant principle" and "Catholic substance." He strongly insists that the two are interdependent, each unable to live without the other. By the Protestant principle he means the principle of criticism, the willingness to look critically at every human power, doctrine, or institution. Without continual criticism, powers and institutions tend to place themselves beyond criticism and take on the status of gods. Yet mere criticism by itself levels everything before it. This seems to have happened in some corners of official Christendom. In violent reaction against Puritan and Victorian theologies and life patterns, these "prophets" direct theological criticism at almost all existing patterns of the Christian life. No new pattern or piety is forthcoming, yet faith needs *some* pattern of concrete expression. What is left is simply the pattern of criticism itself. A pattern is thereby produced that is primarily reactive, a pattern of sophisticated, intellectual, and theologically grounded cynicism. The heroes of this piety are the prophet Amos and the prophet Kierkegaard. The Christian life consists in critical and "prophetic" activity against all plans, claims, and movements.

I do not want to attempt a blanket criticism of such "prophetism." Any given instance of it may be valid and necessary. I only want to point out that the total phenomenon functions as one of the substitute pieties that have arisen to fill the empty house left by Protestant piety. Furthermore, even though it has all the marks of a "religious" piety, it cannot function as a genuine piety. Because it tries to function as a piety, it is not real prophetism. Prophetic criticism intends solely to mediate the Word of God, forthtelling God's Word to a situation. Pious theological cynicism functions primarily to fill a vacuum. God may, of course, use it and speak his Word through it. But the total phenomenon itself is not necessarily a mediation of God's Word. This is why it is "empty" prophetism. Nor is it a genuine piety, because it does not provide an organizing pattern of the Christian life in the sense of any constructive directive. If logically followed to the end, cynical criticism must turn on itself, and the result would be a paralyzing nothingness. Samuel Butler gives us a delightful portrayal of this piety in his poem *Hudibras,* the Presbyterian Knight:

> As if Religion were intended
> For nothing else but to be mended:
> A sect whose chief devotion lies
> In odd perverse antipathies;
> In falling out with that or this,
> And finding somewhat still amiss.

Closely related to this piety is the more institutional conception of the Christian life as a style of theological study, intellectual struggle, and life in the discussion group. Some departments in official Christendom propose the pattern of regular intellectual inquiry (usually in a group) as the way faith expresses itself concretely. Valuable as this sort of thing may be, it organizes only one aspect of the human being. And it is an institutionally produced phenomenon. After the discussion is over, the question of piety still remains.

The Verbal Piety of "Christian Existentialism"

Perhaps the most all-pervasive piety in official Christendom is a mood or tone that could be called "Christian existentialism." But first some distinctions. Existentialism itself is the name for a *philosophy*. In addition, certain theologians such as Rudolf Bultmann and Paul Tillich have appropriated aspects and insights from this philosophy for their theological work; hence comes *existential theology*. In the present section, I am not talking about either of these primarily intellectual schemes. Rather, the insights and vocabulary of both have produced a certain mood or mind-set in official Christendom at large. This I am calling "Christian existentialism." It means a certain way of conceiving and talking about the Christian life. Therefore, Christian existentialism is one of the several pieties of official Christendom.

The vocabulary of Christian existentialism follows closely the vocabulary of the existentialist theologies. Needless to say, it is very different from the vocabulary of Protestant piety. We hear such words and phrases as man's existential condition," "despair and *angst*," "truth for me," "authentic," "I and Thou meeting," "relevance to man's situation," "persons and things," etc. These phrases resound from pulpits and lecterns; they find their way into church school materials and high-level conferences. They are chattered about in sorority houses, college classes, and centers for campus ministries. They appear to express a new and vigorously alive piety. The main content of these phrases, as they function in official Christendom, is very traditional. The sorts of things this kind of talk is against show why it is traditional. The "Christian existentialist" is suspicious of truth *not* for him, of matters irrelevant to *his* situation. So back we go to Wesley's "truths that tell our hearts forgiven and sighs that waft our souls to heaven." The point seems to be that actual, personal experience of the faith and its realities has priority over doctrines about such. Furthermore, the doctrines about such should be expressions of the existential experiences of faith. This implies that all doctrine and intellectual struggle must pass the test of being "existentially relevant to our condition," able thus to speak to us "where we are."

Because of this great concern with relevance, experiences, encounters, life in community and all that, with such phrases serving as the very air we breathe, the very skin we wear, it sounds as if ours is a very pietistic age. The peculiar thing is that it is not. Does Christian existentialism serve as a genuine piety? The answer is no. In the time of Protestant piety, and especially the period of *pietism* when thousands were "awakening" through the preaching of John Wesley and Jonathan Edwards, there could be talk about religious experiences and its priority because the people really had such experience. The emphasis of official Christendom was not merely verbal. They preached for and expected the hearer's world to break up right there on the spot, and often it did. In contrast, present-day "Christian existentialism" is strangely theoretical. We talk about the importance of despair, relevance, and existential encounter with God, not because we experience these things, but because we think we *ought* to experience them. And we fear down deep that we really do not. This means that the piety of Christian existentialism is mostly a piety of talk. What it means to be a "Christian existentialist" is to talk in a certain way. Christian existentialism is a *religious* pseudo piety in that its intention is to stress Biblical notions of God, the knowledge of God and salvation. But it is not a genuine piety, for its pattern organizes not the Christian life, but rather Christian talk.

A variation on Christian existentialism that moves it a step beyond talk is produced by an alliance with art and literature. The reason this is a step beyond mere talk is that talk about despair, man's condition, etc., occurs in conjunction with some actual experience, namely, the experience of novels, poems, plays, paintings, and works of sculpture. Insofar as these aesthetic media testify movingly to "man's condition," our experience of them might be experience of our own condition. The pattern of piety present here is the pattern of seeking clarification about one's own situation from "existential" art and literature. Presumably, one does not receive forgiveness itself, or redemption, or actual new obedience at the hands of artists and playwrights. That means the real problem of a pattern of genuine piety remains.

The Institutional Piety of Church Renewal

A third piety found in the ranks of official Christendom is not a mood or tone. Its mode of existence is a scheme or plan to "renew" the church. The nature of this piety is some pattern or style of living produced by institutional change. Some of these schemes are so momentous that they can be plotted only by IBM computers and carried out by "task forces." These schemes include ways of getting Christians involved in social problems, the continuing education of ministers, the theological education of laity, the renewal of the liturgy, the revision or elimination of the local church, and the "dialogue" between Christians of different denominations and traditions. The inventors of these schemes do not always intend them to be pieties in the sense of Protestant piety. The point is that these schemes are functioning as substitute patterns and styles of the Christian life in place of traditional Protestant piety.

Furthermore, some of these schemes for the renewal of the church and its life do seem to be intended as pieties, patterns which, if we adopt them, express the Christian life in a "style" appropriate to the twentieth century. Typical writings on these matters usually set forth a gloomy diagnosis of secular pseudo pieties and then give prescriptions for the cure. Berger wants conversion, more theology, more social and political activity, and new institutional forms for the church.[47] Winter wants institutional revision of the church as it exists in suburbia and the central city. He recommends a new *unit* of ministry that would cross the lines between the inner city and suburbia.[48] Further, he proposes centers to train laymen theologically and in civic responsibility preparing them for massive attacks on racism and other social problems.[49] Marty wants more ecumenical conversation, some changed emphases in the nature of the ministry, and a new architectural setting for the traditional means of grace.[50] Note that these are institutional and sociologically oriented proposals. Related to them are the negative proposals to do away entirely with the institutional church which has now sold out to secularism. Others want to revise the institutional church radically. Horst Symanowski, a pioneering pastor to German industrial society, has found an effective unit of ministry in the house church with laymen as pastors and leaders. The concern of such groups is devoted to the decisions and problems Christians face in their work and in society at large.[51] Proposals to renew the church are now coming forth with seasonal regularity. Some are after the fact. Like Symanowski, their adherents are communicating something that has already been tried successfully; their "proposals" are expressions of existing facts. Others are mostly book and committee proposals: "If only we would do this . . ."

The renewal proposals also have their own in-group lingo, especially those which are proposed at conferences, consultations, and in books and articles. One hears plenty about this and that seen "as mission," the "shape" of this and that, having "dialogue" with this and that, and "involvement" in this and that. Note that these proposals are proposals to renew the *church*. How is it that they function as a piety in official Christendom? One matter that occurs to me is that making renewal proposals, or being involved in renewal planning, is itself a pattern of Christian living. Thinking up and carrying out these activities provides a concrete expression for the impulses of faith.

At a second level, insofar as any of these renewal schemes is adopted, the actual lives of Christians would be affected in the sense that new patterns would be introduced. Christians would find themselves organized in small groups, engaged in discussions, or active for some social and political cause. Now I myself am not sure what it means for the church to be "renewed." If it means a rejuvenation of institutional life, perhaps the church will be renewed by schemes like these. But it would still lack a genuine piety. For the question of the organizing pattern of the Christian life still remains after the parish is shaped differently, and after the layman is made a theologian or given a "ministry." Are there any personal and individual goals at all in the Christian life? Are these to be ignored for the sake of social and churchly activities, implying that the Christian can live in fearful or brutal self-deception so long as he is involved in the right things? Do prayer and worship have any point at all? What is the purpose of continual study and intellectual struggle? Is there something called Christian freedom? What does it mean and is it desirable?

Important as the renewal proposals may be, they remain pseudo pieties, since they are *invented* pieties. Can we conceive of Christian piety being produced by a committee or formulated in a book? Can we imagine Christian piety being budgeted, approved by official agencies, typed up by secre-

taries, circulated, criticized, revised, mailed out, and made
available? If not, then renewal proposals cannot measure up
as real substitutes for Protestant piety. The Christian must
have some way to express faith, hence the renewal schemes
may be eagerly received in the church. But since they do not
provide an organizing pattern for the Christian life as such
(only Christian activities), something else will move in and
provide it. The Christian will still be more or less at the
mercy of whatever comes along, especially the loud voices
of the secular pieties and their propaganda machines. That
is our problem in a nutshell. Traditional Protestant piety is
gone, and the only real alternatives facing many Christians
are provided by the secular pieties on the one hand and the
religious pieties on the other. "The last state has become
worse for them than the first."

Chapter Fourteen

BY THE WATERS OF BABYLON

> By the waters of Babylon,
>   there we sat down and wept,
>   when we remembered Zion.
> On the willows there
>   we hung up our lyres.
> For there our captors
>   required of us songs, . . .
> How shall we sing the Lord's song
>   in a foreign land?
>
> *—Psalm 137:1-4*

> And, after all the travail and the stress,
> The mortal struggle and the mortal fear,
> They tumbled up at dawn,
> Sleepy and cursing, damning drink and bread,
> To see before them there,
> Neither the kraken nor the loadstone rock,
> But, thin with distance, thin but dead ahead,
> The line of unimaginable coasts.
>
> *—Stephen Vincent Benét*[52]

Because of the collapse of traditional patterns of obedience that gave meaning to the Christian life, contemporary Christendom, like the exiled Jews, must worship the Lord in a "foreign" age and in a "foreign" land. When the Jews were taken to Babylonia, the forms and institutions that formerly gave particularity to their expressions of faith (the Temple and its cultus, the code of laws for national and economic life) were removed. The Jews were not merely exiled from a territory; they were also exiled from a religious pattern of life. In this sense we, too, live in exile. With traditional Protestant piety gone, and pseudo pieties competing for our energies and activities but unable to fill the vacuum, how can we sing the Lord's song in this foreign land?

The Permanence of Exile

We differ from the exiled Hebrews especially in one important respect. Our exile is in one sense permanent. We cannot go back to Protestant piety. I say this less with relish than with regret. Whatever our criticism of that piety, it was at least a genuine piety.[53] It served to express and make concrete a genuine faith. Its intention at least was Biblical in its interpretation of the Christian life. The issues it struggled with were genuine issues: the possibility of God's Word reaching to the specific level of an act or decision, the possibility of the Word affecting man in his affections or feelings, the importance of motives, and many others. These issues remain, but we cannot return to their Puritan and Victorian expressions.

I do not say this merely because they are vulnerable to theological criticism. Theological criticism has been ignored before and will be ignored again. We cannot return to traditional piety simply because we cannot return to any *one* piety. The many traditions of Christendom (Greek Orthodox, Catholic, Anglican, Calvinist, sect group, African, and Asian) now live before each other in a way that makes it impossible to identify *the* Christian life with any one of them. Christendom has always been comprised of a plurality of traditions. The new feature is that, due to the shrinking of the world and increased ecumenical conversation, these traditions now live before each other and are pushed to acknowledge each other, at least as *Christian* traditions and pieties. Plurality and acceptance of plurality now makes impossible any one Western Protestant phenomenon analogous to traditional Protestant piety. We must recognize and live with the plurality and relativity of pieties. We cannot return to the inflexible provincialism of Protestant piety that knows of and sees only one way to be a Christian.

Nor can we return to the search for individual purity of act and motive at the expense of "guilty" participation in the struggle for power. This is not to say that questions as to what I shall do and be are simply eliminated. The exhortations to social activism are addressed to the individual, and they assume that engaging in social and political struggles is something appropriate to the being of the individual. They imply that *one* of the meanings of individual righteousness is active and "guilty" participation in the efforts to better the total human environment of the individual.

The Continuing Structure of Christian Piety

What remains for us who live by the waters of Babylon and who would sing there the Lord's song? Is piety, in every aspect now relativized and dispersed over a pluralism of "styles" of life and "shapes" of parishes, more a matter of taste than necessity? At this point we must make some difficult distinctions. I tried to say in previous chapters that genuine piety is a real expression of Biblical faith. As such it will be an expression of some element in the gospel such as Christian freedom, Christian love, or life in the church. Insofar as every genuine piety is an expression of Biblical faith, it will have certain characteristics. In other words, there is a common, irreducible content and structure in every Christian piety, no matter how different in other respects such pieties are from each other. These common and universal marks of genuine piety should be distinguished from particular historical expressions that will vary from age to age and place to place. Perhaps this distinction is between the indispensable elements in the Christian life and the ever-changing styles or concrete patterns that arise in response to specific situations.

Piety, in the sense of a specific style or organizing pattern, cannot be artificially produced. It cannot be proposed by theologians or thought up in denominational committees. For this reason, no "solution" to the situation described in these chapters can be forthcoming here. The author is in no position to prescribe exactly how to sing the Lord's song in the foreign land. But something can be said about the common or universal aspects of piety, the unavoidable marks of Christian piety wherever it exists. I realize that the brief suggestions that follow may be so much a digest of centuries of theological work and so much a summary of subtle and complicated arguments as to make little sense. I am also aware that this is not an infallible and final word. I do feel responsible for including these suggestions if for no other reason than to provide some criteria by which to measure false and *pseudo* piety. As far as I know, it does represent something of a consensus among Christians who make these matters an object of special concern and inquiry. I would submit the following as the minimum conditions and basic marks of Christian piety wherever it is found, whatever its style.

1. *Revelation as the ultimate source of piety.* Christian piety arises as a response to the demand of God, and this means the God of the Christian gospel. God and his own self-

disclosure is the root and source of genuine piety. Hence, all methods are excluded that proceed merely according to what is useful, pleasurable, practical, or which limit themselves to analyses of human nature or the world. If such matters are ever included, they must in some way be measured by God's revelation.

2. *Specific and concrete directions for being and doing.* No piety is possible unless revelation provides some actual guidance about what is man's "good," what is appropriate to his individual person and society. This element in Christian ethics is what K. E. Kirk calls the element of codification or formalism, and what Edward LeRoy Long terms the casuistical element.[54] Its traditional symbol is the Torah, or Law. In times past this formalist element has threatened to swallow up almost everything else in the Christian life. The sorts of appeals Roman Catholics have traditionally made to "natural law," and the setting forth in Protestantism of rigid and unchanging moral codes, have produced in our times a strong reaction against the whole formalist element. Some writers seem to suggest that piety can do without this element completely. What we cannot forget, however, is that after the criticisms of the formalist element are all in, after our case has been made for human freedom and creativity, after we have observed the historical relativity of this and that law, principle, and custom, we are still left with something called the *human being*. Furthermore, this human being is not merely a nothing. In spite of Jean-Paul Sartre's claim that there is no "human nature," we must observe that if there are human beings, distinguishable from beetles, clocks, and milk shakes, there will be certain things appropriate to the existence, the betterment, even the "destiny" of human beings. Laws, codes, and the like are human attempts to portray certain "structures of appropriateness."

Even when such an element is admitted, it does not settle the question of its status, how such might function in Christian ethics, in what way we can legitimately appeal to it. At least this much is clear. Such structures are not simply synonomous with the Word of God. They have a relativity about them to the degree that one can imagine situations in which they must be bypassed. Such a qualification does not, however, eliminate structures of appropriateness from the Christian life, functioning there as guides, clues, summaries of past wisdom, etc.

3. *The condition of radical transformation.* Christian piety does not comprise the totality or the basis of life under the gospel. For Christian piety (the pattern of the Christian life) is itself the expression of a faith which is prior to it and which makes it possible. Many terms give expression to this: The Christian life proceeds from a "new birth." Good works are "fruits" of justification. The pattern or style of living called "Christian piety" is the expression of the forgiven, freed, and transformed person. In other words, the Christian life is not merely a way of being or doing that is put into effect by will power unrelated to the problem of man's fundamental helplessness and slavery to sin. The Christian life is not so much a seeking, a quest, an inquiry, or a discipline as it is a giving-expression-to, an overflowing, a consequence. Hence, joy, praise, and thanksgiving are more adequate descriptions of the direction of piety than resolution, striving, and tension.

4. *The conjunction of a contemporaneous Word and present decision.* Since the Christian life is life under a present demand of a living God, it can never be seen merely as obedience to laws fixed in the past. Hence, the typical question of Christian piety is not, What is in the law or the tradition? Rather, it is, What response must now be made to God as he speaks at the conjunction of past wisdom, the present situation, and my own decision?

5. *The context of a social and historical environment.* The Christian life is always lived in a situation that includes various human communities and environments: the world

situation as a whole, the neighborhood, the place of work, the family, the church. Therefore, Christian piety can never be reduced to the individual concern of how I can be pure. Its more typical type of response is: What does so and so need? What response does this situation warrant?

6. *The demand of a rigorous discipline.* The situation of the Christian life makes heavy demands upon human capacities and powers. Living the Christian life means fighting for causes, shrewdly planning and plotting, interpreting the Christian gospel with a minimum of sentimentality and self-deception. This means that Christian piety does not occur apart from tough-minded intellectual labor and political-social struggle. In short, it requires some kind of self-discipline. This "rigorist" element is the grain of truth in such themes as self-examination, pilgrimage, and religious exercises.

These six marks of Christian piety can, of course, be analyzed in different ways with the list longer or shorter. Such marks would be present in some form wherever Christian piety exists. But they would not themselves constitute a piety, an actual pattern in which the impulses of faith are expressed. If this is the case, perhaps the thesis of these chapters has not gone far enough. Could it be that what has collapsed is not merely one historical expression of piety (Protestant piety), but Christian piety itself? For does there exist now a piety which genuinely bears these marks?

The six elements seem to be so integral to the Christian life that if any one is eliminated, a significant distortion is effected. When radical transformation is alone emphasized, the Christian life becomes a *pietism,* an exclusive concern with warmness of heart and religious emotions. When rigorous discipline is made prominent, the Christian life becomes a mere moralism. When the contemporaneous Word is alone stressed, the Christian life tends to become an idolatry of the contemporary, tending to ignore past wisdom and

historical sources of revelation. When specific directions are
embraced in isolation, the Christian life tends to generate
into a petty legalism. When the present *context* of church,
world, and nation rules, the Christian life tends to become
a mere imitation of the secular sciences and humanistic wis-
doms.

Enjoying, Working, and Fighting

Can we say anything else about what it may mean to sing
the Lord's song besides stating what are the very general
marks of Christian piety? Let me repeat. No one can just
invent or propose a piety. Yet one further step seems possible. We can make some more specific derivations from the
six elements. If they really are the general elements of the
Christian life, we can be more specific in anticipating certain
ways that faith will express itself at the level of fundamental
attitudes. I would focus on three.

The most prominent fact in the life of the Christian is the
fact of the gospel, the claim that the final word about man
and the world is not a word of condemnation and despair but
a word of grace and hope. The Christian is, of course, aware
of evil in a radical and very terrifying sense. Yet he sees evil
as taken up in the gospel, not vice versa. This means that the
Christian looks upon himself and the world through a particular lens. The world is not only given by God, an expression of God's love and grace; it is still ruled by God and is
the object of God's saving concern. It is even the place where
God "assumed flesh." Now, these rather abstract-sounding
notions are merely attempts on my part to explain a certain
basic attitude that Christians have toward this world, their
total environment which they have at the hands of God. The
deepest and most lasting attitude toward the world is not
resentment but gratitude. Yet this rather static language still
misses the point. Because the Christian sees every event as in
some way a servant of God and because he is beginning to be

free from mere fear and resentment toward these events, the Christian is constantly "alert" and "sensitive" to the world. He sees the future as a realm of surprises, from which come new events, relationships, enjoyments, and tasks.

The point is not so much that the Christian is seeking *experiences* of the world. That would be the opposite of Christian piety, because the self and its experiences would be the real objects of concern rather than the world. Instead, the Christian delights naïvely, almost childishly, in the way spring came this year (not in his *experience* of it), in the wrinkled face of an old woman in the grocery store, in the complexity and mystery of the new employee. "Delight" is perhaps too strong. It seems to say that the Christian responds to every event with the same tone of feeling, which is, of course, nonsense. "Alertness," "curiosity," "wakefulness," the potential and open reception of these events and persons for what they are—would be a more accurate description of it.

While I have not worked this matter through in the way it might be done in the more complete analyses of Christian ethics, my own suspicion at present is that childlike and wakeful enjoyment and alertness to the world is the most fundamental of various attitudes of Christian self-consciousness. For it seems to be the correlate in self-consciousness (to borrow a term from Schleiermacher) of justification by faith. On the negative side, confident alertness toward the unceasing waves of events that come rolling over us drives out a fearful and anxious reception of those events, so that the dominant relation the human being has to finite things is not that of insecurity toward them and an attempt to secure himself by running away from them, or clinging to some one of them for his protection. On the positive side, grateful alertness faces onto the world of objects and events with what Tillich calls the "courage to be." The condemned, guilty, and fearful man tends also to be the paralyzed man, fearing to perceive and understand the world, fearing to act on it and in it with his whole being. Paul's description of the Christian man marching into the future, decked out with the armor of God, portrays a kind of courage that justification creates. Only when events are embraced courageously can they really be enjoyed. Accordingly, they become not mere threats to man's being but occasions of enjoying, working, understanding, creating; in short, occasions for the praise of God through the total being of man in interaction with the world.

When this is the case, the competition between selfishness and unselfishness is no longer the major issue. Alert and spontaneous enjoyment of the self and the world is not a "moral" category in the sense of an ethical principle, the consequence of a moral effort. Since it is the correlate of justification, human works do not produce it. This does not mean that "alert enjoyment" is amoral, totally beyond laws and principles. Rather, the human being, released partially, at least, from fearful and anxious reactions to the world, spontaneously expresses his true being, which is comprised in part of the structures of appropriateness that pertain to his being. Furthermore, alert enjoyment must be the fundamental source of other patterns and attitudes in the Christian life, for this is what impels, guides, and colors responsible acts, forgiveness, compassionate militance, and all the rest.

The opposite of alert enjoyment of the world is imprisonment in the self, where the only matters the person is alert to are interior matters. This is virtually to be without a world. Charles Williams' *Descent Into Hell* portrays this very phenomenon. The "descent" is really a descent into the self, with the world gradually dropping away. To use more traditional language, a person "sins" against this piety when his typical response to the world is that of boredom, finding that which God gives as his environment merely dull, uninteresting, and superfluous.

A second specific attitude of piety could be anticipated from the first. If the Christian sees his environment, his "world," as given to him by God, he will inevitably sense that it is something for which he is responsible. According to the ancient story, the created environment was given to Adam and Eve as something to enjoy, something "pleasant to the sight and good for food" and also something for which they were responsible, something "to till and keep." This responsibility in the world includes responsibility for one's own person, his body, mind, and capacities. This is an abstract way of specifying the attitude of a responsible and competent taking up of one's tasks in the world. For the Christian sees not only his own gifts and capacities but the opportunities of developing and using them in the world as well as a grace. The primary way to be a Christian carpenter is to be a skillful and competent carpenter. The same holds for housewife, lawyer, or laborer. To put it negatively, whenever all sense of responsible response to the world through competent work is lacking, we have a practical, if not theoretical, atheism. I am not talking at this point about the Horatio Alger "virtue" of labor, hard work, carrying one's load, or getting ahead. I am talking, rather, about an attitude that sees work as a responsible response to the world and a competent use of one's capacities as part of that response. A person may work very hard and still work irresponsibly.

While responsibility in the world is more inclusive than simply responsible use of one's gifts in a job, it surely includes that sort of thing. Thomas Wolfe[55] has given us a classic portrayal of a man whose very being could be summarized in the terms "competent and responsible work":

> George found him a curious enigma. Otto Hauser was possessed of remarkable gifts, yet he was almost wholly lacking in those qualities which cause a man to "get on" in the world. In fact, he didn't want to "get on." He had a horror of "getting on," of going any further than he had already gone. He wanted to be a publisher's reader, and nothing more. At James Rodney & Co. he did the work they put into his hands. He did punctiliously what he was required to do. He gave his word, when

he was asked to give it, with the complete integrity of his quiet
soul, the unerring rightness of his judgment, the utter finality
of his Germanic spirit. But beyond that he would not go.

When one of the editors at Rodney's, of whom there were
several besides Foxhall Edwards, asked Hauser for his opinion,
the ensuing conversation would go something like this:

"You have read the manuscript?"

"Yes," said Hauser, "I have read it."

"What did you think of it?"

"I thought it was without merit."

"Then you do not recommend its publication?"

"No, I do not think it is worth publishing."

Or:

"Did you read that manuscript?"

"Yes," Hauser would say. "I read it."

"Well, what did you think of it? (Confound it, can't the
fellow say what he thinks without having to be asked all the
time!)"

"I think it is a work of genius."

Incredulously: "You *do!*"

"I do, yes. To my mind there is no question about it."

"But look here, Hauser—" excitedly—"if what you say is
true, this boy—the fellow who wrote it—why, he's just a kid—
no one ever heard of him before—comes from somewhere out
West—Nebraska, Iowa, one of those places—never been anywhere, apparently—if what you say is true, we've made a discovery!"

"I suppose you have. Yes. The book is a work of genius."

"But— (Damn it all, what's wrong with the man anyway?
Here he makes a discovery like this—an astounding statement
of this sort—and shows no more enthusiasm than if he were
discussing a cabbage head!)—but, see here, then! You—you
mean there's something wrong with it?"

"No, I don't think there's anything wrong with it. I think it
is a magnificent piece of writing."

"But—(Good Lord, the fellow *is* a queer fish!)—but you
mean to say that—that perhaps it's not suitable for publication
in its present form?"

"No. I think it's eminently publishable."

"But it's overwritten, isn't it?"

"It *is* overwritten. Yes."

"I thought so, too," said the editor shrewdly. "Of course, the fellow shows he knows very little about writing. He doesn't know how he does it, he repeats himself continually, he is childish and exuberant and extravagant, and he does ten times too much of everything. We have a hundred other writers who know more about writing than he does."

"I suppose we have, yes," Hauser agreed. "Nevertheless, he is a man of genius, and they are not. His book is a work of genius, and theirs are not."

"Then you think we ought to publish him?"

"I think so, yes."

"But—(Ah, here's the catch, maybe—the thing he's holding back on!)—but you think this is all he has to say?—that he's written himself out in this one book?—that he'll never be able to write another?"

"No. I think nothing of the sort. I can't say, of course. They may kill him, as they often do—"

"(God, what a gloomy Gus the fellow is!)"

"—but on the basis of this book, I should say there's no danger of his running dry. He should have fifty books in him."

"But—(Good Lord! What *is* the catch?)—but then you mean you don't think it's time for such a book as this in America yet?"

"No, I don't mean that. I think it *is* time."

"Why?"

"Because it has happened. It is always time when it happens."

"But some of our best critics say it's not time."

"I know they do. However, they are wrong. It is simply not their time, that's all."

"How do you mean?"

"I mean, their time is critic's time. The book is creator's time. The two times are not the same."

"You think, then, that the critics are behind the time?"

"They are behind creator's time, yes."

"Then they may not see this book as the work of genius which you say it is. Do you think they will?"

"I can't say. Perhaps not. However, it doesn't matter."

"Doesn't *matter!* Why, what do you mean?"

"I mean that the thing is good, and cannot be destroyed. Therefore it doesn't matter what anyone says."

"Then—Good Lord, Hauser!—if what you say is true, we've made a great discovery!"

"I think you have. Yes."

"But—but—is that *all* you have to say?"

"I think so, yes. What else *is* there to say?"

Baffled: "Nothing—only, I should think *you* would be excited about it!" Then, completely defeated and resigned: "Oh, *all* right! *All* right, Hauser! Thanks very much!"

The people at Rodney's couldn't understand it. They didn't know what to make of it. Finally, they had given up trying, all except Fox Edwards—and Fox would never give up trying to understand anything. Fox still came by Hauser's office—his little cell—and looked in on him. Fox's old grey hat would be pushed back on his head for he never took it off when he worked, and there would be a look of troubled wonder in his sea-pale eyes as he bent over and stooped and craned and stared at Hauser, as if he were regarding for the first time some fantastic monster from the marine jungles of the ocean. Then he would turn and walk away, hands hanging to his coat lapels, and in his eyes there would be a look of utter astonishment.

3.

A third specific expression of Christian piety sounds like a contradiction. For want of a better name, I would call it compassionate militance. The kind of world we live in is a world of continually developing problems and challenges that come forth from our natural and social environments. This is further complicated by the fact that ours is a "bent" world, a world marred by malice, ignorance, and a network of evil. It is a world in which simply to capitulate is to turn matters over to "principalities, . . . powers, . . . the world rulers of this present darkness." The Christian cannot be a Christian (one for whom the most prominent fact is the gospel) in such a situation without constant fighting. What is he fighting for? Not simply for religion or the church. The

Christian is fighting wherever and whenever human welfare is at stake. He fights tyranny, prejudice, poverty, superstition, panic, crime, and just plain silliness. He fights in church, in the union, at the office, at the plant, in the professional association, in the bureaucracy, and in the neighborhood. He fights through teaching his children, giving money and withholding money, voting, reading the newspapers, writing letters, working for the party, and attending boring meetings. He fights in humor, shrewdness, anger, and compassionate love. He knows that sometimes he may fight on the wrong sides and in the wrong ways. These are simply the risks he must take, for fight he must.

Even if the problem of Christian piety were solved, and we were suddenly given a new and neatly wrapped package, the last word would not be spoken. For piety is not the last word or even the first. The question always remains about the *status* of piety, and the attitude we have toward piety. It is possible to have the same piety but in different ways. For how do we view these patterns of alertness, competent work, and compassionate militance, or the specific "style" in which these attitudes express themselves? Are we destroyed if they fail or lack perfection? Do they separate us from our brothers? Do they manipulate God? Such questions reveal the limitations and terrible dangers in every piety. Before and after piety must be the good news of Jesus Christ in which we are to "live and move and have our being."

Notes

NOTES

1. Dietrich Bonhoeffer, *The Cost of Discipleship* (The Macmillan Company, 1948).

2. The reader may recognize that this emphasis on the "neutral" nature of piety is a departure from traditional meanings of piety. Traditionally, the only alternatives were piety and impiety. Piety therefore was a word like "justice," meaning always something good and to be desired. In this series, it is a more neutral word, such as "act," for example, which can be either good or bad.

3. For instance, see John Calvin's "On the Christian Life," and also The Westminster Confession of Faith, Chs. XVI, XIX, and XXI. The reader will recall the phrase in the frequently used prayer of confession "That we may hereafter live a godly, righteous, and sober life."

4. We are therefore distinguishing "Protestant piety" from what is called "Pietism." Historically, Pietism was a movement among European Protestant Christians of the seventeenth century that marked a return to the experiental aspects of the Christian faith. Pietism was suspicious of the Scholastic debates of the orthodox theologians. Its proponents stressed, rather, the devotional life, individual exercises designed to procure holiness. Although its founder was Philipp Jacob Spener (1635–1705), Pietism actually spread through the Moravians, led by Count von Zinzendorf, through the preaching ministry of John Wesley, and through the Great Awakening in America. Theologically speaking, Pietism is an interpretation of the Christian faith that unifies everything

under the one notion of Christian piety, instead of, for instance, justification by faith.

5. Graham Greene, *The End of the Affair* (The Viking Press, Inc., 1951).

6. By Percy Dearmer (1867–1936).

7. *Advice to a Young Christian* (G. & C. & H. Carvill, 1830), p. 156.

8. From a song of the early twentieth century, quoted in *Enthusiasm: A Chapter in the History of Religion,* by R. A. Knox (Oxford University Press, 1950), p. 570.

9. H. Richard Niebuhr, *The Purpose of the Church and Its Ministry* (Harper & Brothers, 1956), pp. 44–45.

10. Tom Driver, "Epitaph for an Epic," *The Christian Century,* November 1, 1961, pp. 1302–1303.

11. James Whitcomb Riley, "Equity—?" from *The Complete Poetical Works of James Whitcomb Riley* (Grosset & Dunlap, Publishers), p. 654.

12. Søren Kierkegaard, *Fear and Trembling* (A Doubleday Anchor Book, 1954).

13. George Orwell, *A Clergyman's Daughter* (Harcourt, Brace and World, Inc.), p. 211.

14. *Advice to a Young Christian,* passim.

15. In Georgia Harkness, *Religious Living* (Association Press, 1937).

16. Leslie D. Weatherhead, *How Can I Find God?* (Fleming H. Revell Company, 1934), p. 84.

17. James Baldwin, *The Fire Next Time* (The Dial Press, 1963), p. 49.

18. Jonathan Edwards, *Treatise Concerning the Religious Affections* (The Banner of Truth Trust, 1961), p. 29.

19. "Sinners, Obey the Gospel Word," from the 1780 Methodist *Hymnbook,* quoted from unpublished lectures on hymnody by Norman Langford. Italics added.

20. Quoted in Norman Langford, *loc. cit.,* p. 49.

21. See Gibson Winter, *The Suburban Captivity of the Churches* (Doubleday & Company, Inc., 1961).

22. *The Hymnbook,* Hymn 318.

23. David Head, *He Sent Leanness: A Book of Prayers for the Natural Man* (The Macmillan Company, 1959).

24. William Miller, *Piety Along the Potomac* (Houghton Mifflin Company, 1964), p. 29.

25. Reinhold Niebuhr, *Leaves from the Notebooks of a Tamed Cynic* (Meridian Books, The World Publishing Co., 1957), p. 118.

26. Clifton E. Olmstead, *Religion in America: Past and Present* (Prentice-Hall, Inc., 1961), p. 112.

27. Gayraud S. Wilmore, *The Secular Relevance of the Church* (The Westminster Press, 1962), p. 43.

28. Dietrich Bonhoeffer, *The Cost of Discipleship* (The Macmillan Company, 1961), p. 36.

29. From "Mad as the Mist and Snow," *The Collected Poems of William Butler Yeats* (The Macmillan Company, 1953), p. 261.

30. Jules Feiffer, *Sick, Sick, Sick* (McGraw-Hill Book Company, Inc., 1958).

31. G. K. Chesterton, *Manalive* (Thomas Nelson & Sons, 1912), p. 330.

32. For instance, see James Ussher's definition of worldliness and flesh in *A Body of Divinitie* (London, 1646), pp. 335–336.

33. Richard Hunter, unpublished letter, Spring, 1964, used by the author's permission.

34. Dietrich Bonhoeffer, *Prisoner for God* (The Macmillan Company, 1954), pp. 168–169.

35. C. S. Lewis, *The Screwtape Letters* (The Macmillan Company, 1945).

36. G. K. Chesterton, *What's Wrong with the World:* With a Tutorial Introduction by F. J. Sheed (Sheed & Ward, Inc., 1942), p. 15.

37. C. S. Lewis, *The Screwtape Letters*, p. 112 and p. 68.

38. John Bunyan, *The Pilgrim's Progress* (Fleming H. Revell Company, 1903), pp. 55–56.

39. *The Hymnbook*, Hymn 298.

40. Examples of similar classics in Catholic literature that describe the goal and the "means" of attaining it would be Thomas à Kempis, *Imitation of Christ*, Ignatius of Loyola, *Spiritual Exercises*, and Francis of Sales, *Introduction to the Devout Life*.

41. For this and similar notions, the author is indebted to H. Richard Niebuhr's posthumously published work, *The Responsible Self* (Harper & Row, Publishers, Inc., 1963). In this

work, one of the most eminent of Protestant moral theologians in the present day raises the question whether or not the "teleological" or "pilgrimage" way of looking at the Christian life is the only way.

42. Matthew Arnold, from "Dover Beach" and "The Scholar-Gipsy" in *Eminent British Poets of the 19th Century*, ed. P. L. Lieder (Harper & Brothers, 1938), Vol. II, p. 396.

43. Will Herberg's *Protestant—Catholic—Jew* (Doubleday & Company, Inc., 1955) was one of the first such studies. He ingeniously traced the emergence of an "American religion" to the way America functioned as a melting pot for Jewish, Catholic, and Protestant immigrant groups. Martin Marty gives a clear summary of this new cultural religion in his book *The New Shape of American Religion* (Harper & Brothers, 1959) and also in *Second Chance for American Protestants* (Harper & Row, Publishers, Inc., 1963). A. Roy Eckardt summarized the cultural and secular nature of the so-called "religious revival" of the 1950's in *The Surge of Piety in America* (Association Press, 1958), and William Lee Miller applied the same observation to the political scene in the Eisenhower years in articles now published in *Piety Along the Potomac* (Houghton Mifflin Company, 1964). The sociological dimension of American cultural religion is described in Gibson Winter's *The Suburban Captivity of the Churches* (Doubleday & Company, Inc., 1961) and *The New Creation as Metropolis* (The Macmillan Company, 1963), and also in Peter L. Berger's *The Noise of Solemn Assemblies* (Doubleday & Company, Inc., 1961).

44. See H. Steigman's review of *None Dare Call It Treason* in *The Congressional Record*, September 10, 1964, for a detailed report of the way in which one influential book from the superpatriot literature employed "documentation."

45. C. S. Lewis, *That Hideous Strength: A Modern Fairy-Tale for Grown-ups* (The Macmillan Company, 1946).

46. Joyce Cary, *The Horse's Mouth* (Harper & Brothers, 1944).

47. Berger, *op. cit.*

48. Winter, *Suburban Captivity*.

49. Winter, *The New Creation as Metropolis*.

50. Marty, *The New Shape of American Religion*.

51. Horst Symanowski, *The Christian Witness in an Industrial*

Society, tr. by George H. Kehm, with an Introduction by Robert B. Starbuck (The Westminster Press, 1964).

52. Stephen Vincent Benét, *The Western Star* (Farrar & Rinehart, Inc., 1943), pp. 12–13.

53. See H. Richard Niebuhr, *The Kingdom of God in America* (Willett, Clark & Co., 1937), for a historical documentation of the serious and genuine nature of traditional Protestant piety in its American expression.

54. K. E. Kirk, *The Vision of God* (Longmans, Green & Co., Inc., 1931), and Edward LeRoy Long, Jr., *Conscience and Compromise* (The Westminster Press, 1954).

55. Thomas Wolfe, *You Can't Go Home Again* (Harper & Brothers, 1940), pp. 22–25.

In reply to myth, false liberty — that I have to try everything for myself before I can be whole! All religions, all sensory experience, etc. all questions, answers before I can be a Chr. — — Is it so that I cannot experience health – being well – until I have had every disease? There may be an infinite # but I need to taste them all to know health? Nonsense. Apart from fact that many of them will forbid me from ever having health but rather death; is the fact that I can know health without ever being ill. (true illness makes me appreciate health more) So don't fall for that one — drugs, sex, gurus, etc – before I can come to myself. Many never find their way back or thru.

Temptation consists of desire and curiosity — perhaps with the latter predominating. It is a drive for a thrill in response to a variety of inner impulses. It is heedless of consequences, and is actually motivated by danger; risk. A woman's love can even steal a man away from God, they say.

Loneliness, it has been said, is the fear of love. Sometimes; Sometimes it is the unfulfilled want of it.

109 & empty prophetesses today)